GOOD SEXUAL HYGIENE
and
SPIRITUAL ATTITUDE

ANTHONY ALEXANDER MORRIS

ISBN 978-1-0980-6297-2 (paperback)
ISBN 978-1-0980-6298-9 (digital)

Christian Faith Publishing, Inc.
832 Park Avenue
Meadville, PA 16335
www.christianfaithpublishing.com

Cover image: MNStudio/shutterstock

BASAC subject codes:
HEA042000   HEALTH & FITNESS/ Sexuality
MED102000   MEDICAL/ Mental Health
YAN051200   YOUTH ADULT NONFICTION/ Social
                        topics/ Self-Esteem & Self-Reliance
TEC029000   TECHNOLOGY   &   ENGINEERING/
                        Operations Research
REL028000   RELIGION / Ethics

Printed in the United States of America

Contents

Note to Reader

This book is a counseling aid on spiritual ethics, sexuality, and health with advice to improve your moral attitude. It packs the potential to benefit people of all ages and can help everyone develop a desire to live by good ethical values. I have included many true stories from my own experience to help illustrate some of the concepts.

I reserve the right to not answer any questions, clarify any statements, interpret or explain any of the feelings contained within these pages.

All thoughts, views, and life experiences expressed within are mine and mine alone and, as such, are accountable to no one, nor are they to be interpreted by anyone.

Introduction

Good Sexual Hygiene and Spiritual Attitude was written to help adults, parents, and children gain a better understanding of each other. It was also written to help make your marriage work or, hopefully, restore your marriage.

In today's society, there are many concerns that both parents and teenagers encounter which seem to go unnoticed because of the generation gap between them. When people are aware of these concerns, those of different ages often have very different views on them. This book covers many areas where myths or idle preferences obscure the truth and the consequences of wrong choices.

This book also looks at some ridiculous ancient social customs related to sexuality that are still rigidly practiced by most societies today, creating a lot of unhealthy attitudes between parents and their children. There appears to be a great deal of respect and harmony between parents and teens where the ancient social customs this book exposes are not practiced.

A number of dramatic and unique experiences have impacted my life, helping me to see what really is responsible for the generation gap frustrations. One was a lecture I received at the age of sixteen from a woman who overheard a remark I made to her son about using girls as casual sex toys. It infuriated her so much that she ended up lecturing us for over three hours about having a mature sexual attitude. It was an important lesson on how to live in purity of spirit and body instead of becoming a sexually irresponsible and immoral person destined for disappointment.

Our beliefs about our sexuality affect every other aspect of our lives. I have pondered observations many people don't seem to ever consider despite the profound impacts on their lives. This book explores subconscious natures that most never see about them-selves, natures which can destroy their life's potential, their marriage, and other relationships.

I hope you will be deeply inspired when you read about the many benefits revealed here, which I believe can enrich your life. *Good Sexual Hygiene and Spiritual Attitude* is an excellent source of instruction for every-one. It is very useful in helping parents understand hidden stresses their children endure but don't know how to explain to adults. It emphasizes how the practice of good spiritual and sexual habits will greatly reduce the frustrating risk of becoming a victim of sex-related diseases, the regrets of sexual molestation, the risks associated with escaping to drugs or gangs, etc. This book exposes the guts of these problems and gives simple solutions to resolve the frustration.

It's never too late to change once you know what you need to do.

Some of the doctrine is very bluntly stated, as though it is giving you a serious talking to, and it is. Simple illustrations from true stories are used as well to express the importance of practicing good sexual hygiene and spiritual attitudes.

One last thought to leave with you: when you fly over a country, you learn very little about it. However, if you walk through that country, you learn far more. Speed-reading this material will result in little (if any) benefit to you. So read *Good Sexual Hygiene and Spiritual Attitude* with a concern to get a thorough understanding of its relevance.

What Is Sex?

The laws of nature can't be changed to suit anyone's personal desired preferences. Nature can't be bribed. And nature is indifferent to the cost of ignorance. Therefore, no matter how much you think you know about sexuality, it is important to read this chapter because it sets a mood for the following chapters to help you understand the purpose of their content.

Even the most honest and confident parents can feel uneasy about discussing sex with their children, in part, because pagan taboos have created shame about human sexuality. When a child asks, "Where did I come from?" many parents talk around or completely change the subject because they don't want to discuss it with their children. This leaves our children confused and having to find out for themselves.

By providing our children with open, honest, and realistic communication from birth, we encourage them to also be open and honest with us. Even when they bring up difficult subjects such as sex, encourage them to ask questions and try to provide satisfactory answers. This will provide them with a good, strong foundation.

After reading this chapter, you can decide whether or not it conflicts with your ideas on teaching your child about sex.

So You Want to Know Where You Came From

The short answer to that is: from your parents, but that does not answer your question properly at all. To understand where you came from and what sex has to do with where you came from, first you need to know something about how your body works.

All body parts are the same in boys and girls except their sex organs. The sex organs determine whether you are of the male gender (boys) or the female gender (girls). Both male and female people have legs, arms, a head, a chest cavity, and a stomach area. Also, both genders have vital life-supporting organs that are the same and are essential for life, like your heart and lungs, your liver, and kidneys.

Most organs work in a specialized system. One example is the respiratory system. It consists of your nose, mouth, throat, windpipe, and lungs, which work together to get oxygen from the air for the body. The respiratory system cooperates with the circulatory system, which carries the oxygen from the lungs to every one of the billions of cells of your body.

Another example is your digestive system, which begins with your mouth to take in and chew your food. Your esophagus carries that food to your stomach, which further breaks down the food to get the nutrients ready to be absorbed through your small intestine and large intestines and into the circulatory system, which carries nutrients (along with oxygen) to all the cells of your body. And finally, your rectum gets rid of the waste, the leftover material not absorbed to feed your body.

All the required organ systems for your body to live are complete in your body.

The sex organs form the reproduction system, which produces babies. Unlike the other systems, the sexual organ systems of a male and female are different and *incomplete* in either gender and must work together to perform their function. In other words, to produce babies, the reproductive system of one person must depend on an association with organs from a person of the other gender.

The reproductive system also must grow up, or mature, before it can produce life. (Similarly, babies must grow up to become young men and women before they are mature enough to look after themselves and others.)

When a female baby is born, she carries all of her ova or egg cells that can produce babies in her ovaries. (One of the eggs, or ova, by itself is called an ovum.) However, none of these ova can produce babies until after she reaches her adolescent years, when her menstrual cycles begin (usually between age ten to sixteen); and they will not produce babies unless they are fertilized.

When a male reaches adolescence, his body is capable of producing sperm cells that can stimulate the ova in a female to grow into babies. This stimulating process is called fertilization.

We can think of fertilization as adding the missing part (ingredient) that is needed to start it growing or working. It is somewhat like adding water to a seed to make it grow. Or we can think of it as a car which needs fuel to energize it and a key to start it. In each example, something must be added to make it grow or start.

Normally, in each female, one ovum each month becomes ready for fertilization. The female's body prepares a place for the fertilized egg to grow by using nutrient-rich blood to create a special lining in the uterus, which is also called a womb. If the egg is not fertilized, the lining and the egg are shed from her body in a process called menstrual flow.

This monthly cycle repeats itself until an ovum is fertilized, resulting in pregnancy. (After pregnancy, the cycle resumes until the female reaches menopause, which varies from age thirty-five to fifty-eight. When menopause is completely finished, the woman can no longer become pregnant.)

Sexual fertilization starts the growth of a baby and gives the child features that look somewhat like their fathering parent and somewhat like their mother. The baby's genes come from the combined genes they inherit from their birth parents. The sexual organ systems of a man's and a woman's bodies must work together to make one complete sexual organ system to produce their offspring.

The cycle of birth begins in the testicles of the fathering parent. The testicles are glands which produce millions of tiny sperm cells. These are the father's reproductive cells. The sperm cells mix with fluids from the prostate and bulbourethral (bəl-(ˌ) bō-yu̇-ˈrē-thrəl) glands to make a thick, milky-looking secretion called semen. The sperm cells look like tadpoles swimming around in this solution. However, they are so small that a microscope is needed to see them.

The male sexual organ system is stimulated in much the same way as the saliva glands in your mouth are stimulated. When you think of food that is delicious to eat, it causes an increased flow of saliva; your mouth waters.

When the male is thinking of a female he feels affectionate love for, his sexual organs are stimulated. This causes the artery blood vessels in his penis to dilate. The dilated arteries cause an increased volume of blood to flow into the muscular tissues of his penis. This pressure buildup is assisted by the veins, restricting their drainage flow back toward the heart. Thus, the penis's muscular tissue becomes engorged with blood, which causes it to inflate and lengthen (somewhat like a balloon filling with air) to become a firm shaft. When a male's penis is stimulated in this way, it is called an erection.

The penis of the fathering parent and the vagina of the mothering parent are the indicating difference between a male and a female and are designed to fit together. To do this, the male must become stimulated to produce an erection. This is necessary so a male can penetrate his penis into the vault of his female partner's vagina. This process is called copulation or sexual intercourse. By this connected passage, the semen solution carrying sperm cells is safely transferred from his body to hers.

However, this does not usually happen automatically upon sexual contact of the connected sexual organs. A reciprocating action of the male's erection sliding in and out in a somewhat repetitive motion further arouses stimulation until involuntary muscle contractions start in the male's reproductive system. (An example of involuntary contractions is hiccups. You can't control when they will happen.) The involuntary contractions of the male's sex organs work like a pump, safely injecting semen deep into the female's vagina. This muscle contraction of the male's sexual organs is called ejaculation.

The transferred sperm cells in the semen solution swim to the womb of the female's body. To further assist the sperm cells to reach their destination, the female's sexual organs also are stimulated. The reciprocating action of the connected sexual organs induces sensations in her body to secrete fluid into the vaginal vault to dilute the thick semen solution. This makes it easier for the sperm cells to swim to the ovum (or egg cell), which is waiting near the ovary. Only one out of these thousands of sperm cells will unite with the ovum to produce a fertile embryo.

The embryo travels from the fallopian tube to the female's uterus, where it develops into a baby.

In the latter stages of development, when the embryo starts to take on the look of a baby, it is called a fetus. However, from the time of inception/pregnancy, it is a live human that is developing into a baby.

Sometimes, more than one ovum is ready for fertilization, and sometimes a single embryo develops into more than one baby, resulting in twins or even more babies all developing at the same time.

Since babies develop in the female's body, there are more extensively developed sex organs in her body than there are in the male's body. However, neither a man nor a woman can produce a baby without the assistance of the other one because both must work together to make one complete sex organ system.

The mother's uterus provides nourishment, warmth, and protection while the baby develops over the next nine months. At the time the baby no longer needs its mother's internal assistance to live and grow, the baby is ready to be born.

To be born means to come out after being developed. An example of this is a car factory. All that is required to make the cars and support the factory is brought to it as material and energy supplies that feed the system. With the materials, energy is used to assemble the cars.

However, the cars can't go on their own while being assembled because they are not fully developed yet. After the cars are assembled, they are ready to come out and go on their own without the support of the factory. In much the same way, a mother takes in nourishment to support her own energy needs and the energy needs of the baby that is developing inside her body.

The interaction when a male and female are together is called coitus, but it is better known as sexual intercourse. The function of sexual intercourse is not spontaneous. It is the result of a mental decision of cooperation between a man and a woman. Thus, the interaction of sexual intercourse only happens when they want it to happen. That is the way God designed us so all children would have a father and a mother as parents to look after them.

The Importance of a Good Beginning

When the baby is ready to be born, it is a very exciting time for the parents, especially if it is their first child because it is the beginning of the biggest step of their lives. The parents of a child are the woman who is the mother and the man who fathered the baby by providing sperm to fertilize the ovum. This is a shared responsibility of the love they hopefully have for each other. It is the priceless gift of a new life from their own bodies for them to invest their future into. It is their gift to each other.

Parents are supposed to care for and look after their children until they are grown up into mature adults, until they can take care of themselves and any children they may have. However, all too often, those who have reached adolescence and are able to have children do not take proper care of them. And yet everyone *knows* they should by the guilt that they feel deep inside when they consider escaping the responsibility of looking after their children.

Sexual intercourse is also known as making love or having sexual pleasure with another person of the opposite sex. This is the main reason men and women are attracted to each other: to become married partners and live the rest of their lives together before and after becoming parents

However, to really be making love to another person requires far more than consenting to share sexual pleasure. It demands a lifetime of commitment to being a clean, responsible, and honorable person for your spouse (marriage partner) and any children you may have. The biblical law from the Almighty Creator of the universe indicates that when a man and woman live together they should be as husband and wife. They should commit themselves to looking after each other and their children.

The privilege of sexual relationship is a very serious responsibility. It is not to be considered lightly, just as being in control of a car or an airplane is a serious responsibility. You can see the joy of being able to drive a car or fly a plane long before you can drive or fly. This is so because first you must qualify for a license. To qualify, you must prove to an examiner that you are mature enough and skilled enough to handle the vehicle safely. Similarly, it takes time training to manage the responsibilities that go with the license of marriage and with raising children.

To train yourself for marriage, you must want to develop a mature attitude. That means taking a stand to be obedient to good and responsible advice from your parents and teachers. You also need to finish your schooling, *grow to wisely appreciate the value of constructive criticism,* and learn how to work.

Also, you should learn the responsibilities of living such as controlling yourself and being able to get along with other people in all types of situations.

Then will come the biggest test of all. You need to experience standing alone for what is right when your peers are trying to convince you to do wrong. Only then will you be a well-seasoned mature individual able to manage the responsibilities of marriage and appreciate its rewards.

The Most Rewarding Choice

A good rewarding marriage demands a lot of hard work, dedication, and having a caring heart for others.

Shirking the responsibilities that should go along with sexual intimacy will cause grief that far out-weighs the short-lived pleasures from coitus. Sincere companionship, security, and trust are values we all long for more than gold. Live together with a sworn vow to live for each other. Otherwise, you will want to leave yourself a convenient and irresponsible way out.

Is your love sincere, or is it something fleeting that is here today and gone tomorrow when problems come up as they will?

There is a good spiritual way to live as a male or female that bestows blessed sexuality in our lives. This way will make your life the happy one the Creator of the universe wants us to enjoy. This we know from the tranquility of natural beauty we experience when we are out in any unspoiled wilderness area of nature.

Other choices take us in a different direction where we can live an irresponsible dirty life, the type of life that the evil influences of immoral sexuality try to lure us to desire. By the corruption around us, we can see man has promoted a lot of indecent adulterous attitudes as the way to enjoy life. However, the inner spirit in us knows it is wrong. Consider with sensible judgment the tempting insane stress associated with pornography and prostitution. Tempting illusions are put before us to shatter our good moral spirit. We face their enticing stress every day in the polluted world that man has made for himself. The stress to indulge in evil encourages us to give up our good moral beliefs. The commercialized overbearing influential traits of the society we live in make the good appear to be undesirable and the bad to look appealing.

Haters of loving kindness and goodness will try to make the bad look good and desirable. They try to persuade us to think the wrong time for sexual relations is the right time. However, capitulating to this temptation always causes unhappiness and regret and often emotional and medical problems as well. Immoral sex at any time, or passionate love at the wrong time, has shattered many young adults' futures—sometimes beyond hope of recovery.

Because the Bible contains many wise statements that have been medically proven to be preventive advice and protection against becoming a victim of bad choices, I like to think of it as an operating manual from the Creator. By staying loyal to its instructions, we can avoid the painful results of impulsive temptation-driven behavior.

One of the instructions says, "If you really sincerely love someone and desire to have sexual intercourse with that person, then marry him or her first." We can say we believe this or that about sex before marriage. However, because of our deep down sense of the truth and what's right, we feel uneasy about the rightfulness of sexual intimacy without first being married.

After some time of indulging in sex before marriage, some of those practicing this become calloused against the sensed immorality of it. We *forget* the sensed guilt feeling when we repeatedly indulge in any form of immorality; we shut it out as though we are ignorant of it being wrong. As we become comfortable with the practice of an immoral habit, we develop a more accepting attitude toward experiencing more degenerate sexual conduct. With this in mind, we should try to avoid all immoral practices because it always ends up destroying happiness in a relationship.

Those who prepare themselves throughout their youth to be well-seasoned mature individuals who understand their moral responsibilities live much happier lives. In marriage, they survive and recover from hardships much better, especially if they are with a mature responsible mate because they are a united front. Therefore, everyone should go through all the prerequisites of maturing before marriage. Discipline yourself to abstain from engaging in sexual intercourse before a sincere and responsible marriage to prevent insecure tension. Sincere and responsible people who love one another will dedicate their lives to each other through marriage because they both naturally want to. With this type of dedication, long-term faith becomes established, and the sensed threat of unhappiness is removed.

Sex is a factor of the good and bad outcome to practically everything we do in life. Therefore, it is very important for everyone to try and do what is best for all concerned. This is important because sexual intimacy produces babies that need parents to love them for the rest of their lives. That also includes not being a hypocrite or ashamed of discussing the sub-ject of sex with your children.

Explaining sex to your child can be a great bond-ing experience. The subject of sexuality and where babies come from usually leads to technical questions, theirs and yours. It is a very good idea to have a med-ical dictionary on hand to refer to as these questions arise.

What Science Knows About Where We Came From

Some of you may feel a need to put up a resistance to terms like Creator and biblical law. However, I find it impossible to describe our beginning in any other way because of the overwhelming amount of solid scientific evidence that supports the existence of a creator. I find it ludicrous that some scientists still give evolutionary theories any credibility since experiments to prove the authenticity of the evolutionists' evidence have discovered the opposite: not one shred of evidence presented to support evolutionary theory hasn't been exposed to be a fraudulent lie. (Some of the evidence discussed here reflect what I learned from the recorded lectures, "Creation in Symphony" by Dr. Carl Baugh, PhD.).

Creatures of Bone and Tooth

Two powerful pieces of evidence presented to support evolution were the Piltdown Man and the Nebraska Man. Here is a summarized history of their legitimacy:

In 1912, *amateur* archaeologist announced the discovery near Piltdown, East Sussex, England, of a skull which clearly linked man's origin to apes. Although the find met with some controversy at the time, it wasn't until forty-one years later that advanced techniques proved conclusively the Piltdown Man skull was a hoax. New technical forensic equipment revealed that plaster and artificially aged human skull bones had been molded together with the lower jawbone and teeth bones of an ape.

The first reported evidence of an anthropoid primate in America, *Hesperopithecus* (commonly known as the Nebraska Man), consisted of a mere tooth found by rancher Harold Cook in 1917. Cook thought it looked somewhat like a human tooth and something like an ape's tooth and eventually submitted it for scientific examination. Declared in 1922 as evidence of an ape graduating to a man, it was used in 1925 to help win the famous Scopes Trial in Dayton,

Tennessee, and to introduce evolution into the education curriculum that spread worldwide.

But in 1926, Harold Cook went back to the site and dug up the rest of the skeleton, including the jaws. It was found to be an extinct species of pig called *Prosthennops serus*, and in 1927, the earlier identification as an ape was retracted in the journal Science. However, the evolutionary concept has continued to be taught in schools and universities around the world, while any education involving God and the Holy Bible was gradually removed and eventually outlawed from being taught in public schools. Why? It's all salesmanship to promote lies as the truth.

My question is, what is the motive behind governments worldwide dogmatically forcing these blatant lies to be taught to students from then until now? It doesn't matter whether the government is fascist, strong right or left-wing or any political group between them. The clear majority of them have continued to teach evolution in their curriculum.

Creatures of Fire and Flame

Evolutionists argue that the Holy Bible is nothing more than fables. They refer to the statements about a fire-breathing creature named Leviathan in the Bible and say it's impossible. However, science knows that fireflies produce a highly sophisticated chemical reaction in their body to produce the light that we can see at night.

A less-known creature is the bombardier beetle. This small insect is armed with a shockingly impressive defense system that is very closely matched to what a dragon would require to expel fire from its body. Whenever threatened by an enemy attack, these little beetles blast irritating and odious gases at an astonishing 212 degrees Fahrenheit into the face of the unfortunate predator.

To create this dangerously explosive reaction, the beetle stores two chemicals, hydroquinone, and hydrogen peroxide in separate internal chambers. When threatened by a predator, such as a frog, it squirts the chemicals into its tiny reaction chamber, along with other catalyst chemicals, creating violent explosions at hundreds of propulsions per second. With chemicals this dangerous, you can't be experimenting to come up with the perfect solution, you got to first, know what you're doing or you would blow yourself up.

According to evolutionary theory, beetles spent thousands of generations experimenting before arriving at the magic formula, simultaneously developing the "barrel" to aim the mixture at the assailant, along with the intricate muscle tone and finely tuned nervous system to orchestrate the whole defense mechanism safely and with precise accuracy.

Could such a marvelously sophisticated mechanism have evolved haphazardly over millions of years, or was a designer required? And if a designer made the bombardier beetle, it's entirely possible he also made Leviathan, who could now be among the extinct dinosaurs we know existed at one time.

Die-hard evolutionists know the history on the fraudulent evidence used to dismiss creation as fake. They expect you to disregard rational reasoning and dogmatically embrace their theory about our origin even with evidence like the bombardier beetle. Why do they hate the possibility that we were created by a source greater than ourselves? Yet those who do not agree the bombardier beetle *was* capable of gradually developing entirely by itself risk receiving a failing grade in school.

Rock of Ages

Evolutionists proclaim it took three hundred million years for granite to form. Dr. Robert Gentry, an American scientist, examined granite of all colors at all depths of the earth. By carving the rock into thin slices, he showed it is full of halos crystallized (frozen) in a state of radioactive decay, including Polonium 210, 214, and 218.

Polonium, in a state of radioactive decay, goes through seven half-lives and disappears without a trace in a very short period of time. Therefore, it had to crystallize in less time than it would take to go through its seven half-lives for any trace of it being left for us to see. Polonium-210 goes through its seven half-lives in 22 days. So it had to be formed into its crystallized state in less than 22 days to leave any evidence it was there. However, polonium-214 goes through its seven half-lives and disappears without a trace in zero decimal zero zero zero one six four of a second. That's 164 millionths of one second. Therefore, for there to be any trace of it left, it had to form into a crystallized state in *less than 164 millionths of a second.* In other words, it came into existence instantaneously, the way it is described in the Holy Bible in Genesis 1:6–7:

> Then God said, Let there be a firmament in the midst of the waters, and let it divide the waters from the waters. And God made the firmament, and divided the waters

which were under the firmament
from the waters which were above
the firmament and it was so.

Interestingly, the haloes are perfectly round, which means they must have been formed cold—forming hot would have left them distorted.

Scientists worldwide have been aware of these facts about granite for more than two decades, but never a word of it is taught to the general public in schools. Why do they still dogmatically teach that it took three hundred million years for granite to form without any proof? It sounds like a fancy and impressive figure picked at random to impress the gullible against there being a God who created us.

I hope you are sitting down because this next forensic discovery about all living cells is a blockbuster of evidence.

Dr. Denton found cell DNA provides the information for the protein synthesis apparatus *that provides the very proteins for the DNA to exist.* The protein synthesis apparatus provides the protein phosphate compounds for the energy system. *Yet the energy system provides the actual energy for the protein synthesis to function.* The protein synthesis provides the proteins for the cell membrane. *Yet the membrane holds that entire synthesis intact.* In other words, everything is independent and codependent on everything else. All four complex parts of all living cells whether plant or animal had to be complete and perfect from their beginning to ever exist as a living cell, period. Therefore, the forensic evidence proves they had to have been designed by a creator instantaneously to become living cells—God.

Given the evidence, it is surprising how forcefully evolution is proclaimed as truth. This begs the question: How can any proper or sound perspective be taught to students on the subject of human sexuality with such evolutionary lies being saturated into education curriculum worldwide?

Examining the Evidence

If you are interested in finding out more about what science has learned about our creation, get a copy of *Creation in Symphony* from Creation Evidence Museum in Glen Rose, Texas.

If you have any qualms about my stand against evolutionary theories, read the summary article in Science America, October 1994 issue, page 44. There it states that Stephen Weiburg, Ph.D., and Sir Frederick Hoyle, Ph.D., who are two highly respected scientists worldwide, spent over ten years with unlimited funding researching the possibility of evolution occurring by natural means. *Their final conclusion was that there was only one chance in ten to the forty thousandth power for evolution to have happened.* This statement fixes evolution to be thousands of times beyond the realm of anything that is even remotely possible when you compare this fact to the following understood fact about the universe:

Physicists tell us that if the measured universe were filled with electrons, they would number 10 to the 130th power. Therefore, the possibility of picking out a single electron correctly in the entire universe is thousands of times more likely than for evolution to have happened (according to Weiburg and Hoyle's calculations).

With all the millions of experiments done by scientists, the results of which only make sense as the work of an intelligent designer, but some of them still proclaim that a random haphazard mixture of atoms produced simple single cells of life. However, they are still trying to prove that evolution produced *all* the variations of life. The hundreds of millions of dollars spent to acquire the understanding we have today has only resulted in totally fruitless attempts at trying to make life start from nonliving material.

Even with scientists' determination to make this happen, they have not found a shred of evidence to prove life evolved without intelligent intervention. They can't even manipulate an existing mutation organism to produce a characteristic that is not present in its parents and can reproduce a new life-form. They can't make a new species by mutating a species. A mutation does not produce major new raw material. It does not make a new species by altering the structure of a living cell even in the slightest. Stephen J. Gould stated, "I regard the failure to find a clear vector of progress to be the most puzzling factor of the fossil record."

There hasn't even been any evidence detected in all the many varied geological findings in the crust of the earth to support the evolution of life from, as they say, billions of years ago; nor have they found evidence to support the theory that through gradual transformation, species like apes became the man of today.

All scientists *have* found is that *every* complex form of life appears suddenly in time, just as they found, scientifically, granite rock had to have been formed instantaneously, as evidenced by the radioactive polonium-214 found in it. There is no evidence of anything having a transformation time-lapse over any period.

This has led some sincere scientists, who are concerned about working with truthful logic, to stop relying on Darwin's theory of evolution. They have discontinued researching his theory because *more than a hundred years worth of research has not produced one proven evolutionary theory. Instead, every claim has been proven false.* On the other hand, evidence has been found which solidly supports the fact that a mastermind had to exist to create all the life forms that are constructed with atoms.

Sensibly, a growing number of scientists have abandoned the evolutionary theory and have put the creation concept to the test. They have found volumes of undisputable evidence requiring a creator, and there is only one holy book that compares flawlessly with the science: the Holy Bible. It's the only book that gives an accurate account of creation as we see it in nature; and that account is direct, specific, and clear with absolutely no errors found in it despite the thousands of people intent on disproving its authenticity.

The sequence of creation events found in the Holy Bible coincide perfectly with what science knows had to happen to be consistent with the evidence found in nature. Unlike other holy books, the Holy Bible correctly describes the laws of physics. The Holy Bible is also the only book that accurately predicted future events hundreds and even thousands of years before they happened. Therefore, I believe the credibility of the Holy Bible cannot be dismissed as a fictional account of where life came from.

References and suggestions for further reading about this section:

"Hesperopithecus: The first Anthropoid Primate found in America," *Science* 60 (May 5, 1922): 1427, 463.

Henry Fairfield Osborn, "Best Evidence," *Nebraska Man.*

William K. Gregory, "Found to Be A Pig," *Nebraska Man.*

"Hesperopithecus: Apparently Not an Ape nor a Man," *Science* 66 (Dec. 16, 1927): 1770.

"Mutations Are Non-Productive" (lecture at Hobart and William Smith College on Feb. 14, 1980).

Robert V. Gentry, "Polonium Radiohaloes in Granite," Nature 442, Page 282

Stephen J. Gould, "No Clear Vector of Progress," *Natural History* 93 (Feb. 1984), 22–23.

L. B. Halstead, "No Actual Fossils Directly Antecedent to Man," *Nature* (Nov. 20, 1980), 208.

Dr. Michael Denton, *Evolution: A Theory in Crisis* (Bethesda, Maryland: Adler & Adler, 1986), 270.

Logical Conclusions and Practical Application

The advice written in the Holy Bible on sexuality and marriage merits our attention and deserves our respect. It is full of examples promoting living through moral values. Evolution dismisses the need to live by moral values and instead embraces survival of the fittest. It often suggests there are no consequences for indulging in immoral practices; with evolution, there are no laws governing any required conduct. Therefore, there is no penalty for sexual molestation of children or disrespect of females as inferior to men or theft or lying or worse. With evolutionary theory, *all* immoral conduct is simply dismissed as merely the nature of the beast.

However, we *do* know the difference between right and wrong because when doing wrong, we sense uneasiness inside ourselves until, through practice, we desensitize ourselves to it. So what causes us to sense uneasiness in the first place when we start doing immoral things? It is a built-in programmed instinct, isn't it? This becomes evident when we consider some of the science of our existence, like where those instincts come from.

There is a scientific test that you can do to help reason if there is any possibility that creation could have possibly happened. The only apparatus required for this test is your reasoning applied to basic knowledge about the universe that we all have no dispute with already.

One fact science knows to be true about existence is that the source of anything is greater than what it produces. An example of this is people must mature into adults before they're able to produce babies. It takes a pulp mill to produce paper. A crane must be big enough to support a load greater than the load it lifts, and it has to be able to reach higher than the load it lifts up. Therefore, the theory that the source of anything is greater than what it produces makes sense. With this in mind we can look at existence another way. The source of limitless space must be infinite in extent. The source of unbounded variety must be omnipresent in all the phenomena of that variety. And the source of life must be living. How about the source of feelings Ethics and love We could go on and on, but I sum it up in one word—God.

If you are up to taking the challenge, I encourage you to explore Dr. Carl Baugh's lectures, "Creation in

Symphony." He explains why the instinct we *first* feel when we consider doing anything that is not in an act of love and compassion is uneasiness, but the more we ignore that feeling of unease and indulge in doing things that are unloving toward others, the less we will be able to sense we are doing wrong.

The first cause of righteousness must be holy, dedicated to a passion of love, just as you sense when looking at the expression on an innocent baby's face. How far do we stray as we continue listening to brainwashing propaganda to embrace unrighteousness?

With these thoughts in mind, I hope you will not feel offended when you read statements referring to a creator and biblical references as you continue through this counseling book on mankind's sexuality. You may find it quite humorous as you read about some of the struggles I had with these concepts from true stories I witnessed to understanding what is and what is not the right way to live your life.

Summing It Up

The education boards advocate that students need to be taught the fundamental base of our origin (sex education), and I agree on this fact. However, the evolution theory that schools have been teaching is not realistic and therefore is not a rational basis for education about sexuality. They claim that the Holy Bible contradicts itself. However, ongoing research by scholars comparing the scriptures with history, nature and science keeps revealing the narrow-minded scope of our human understanding is the only flaw, not the Holy Bible. Creation by the divine Creator in the Holy Bible is the only concept that has sustained a solid and flawless foundation throughout time.

Therefore, I conclude that the biblical law provided by the Almighty Creator of the universe for our well-being deserves our respect. When it states that a man and woman who live together should be as husband and wife, it is a safeguard. It is a commitment of oath to our Creator that we as marital mates will look after each other and our children for the rest of our lives. Family! And that only makes complete and rational loving sense.

Some words of wisdom from Proverbs 23:23: "Buy the truth and sell it not; not only that, but also get discernment and judgment, instruction and understanding."

Revolution seems to be craved by every coming generation. Someone comes up with an idea and strives to sway people to embrace their new (or revived) way of thinking.

One thing that stunned me was that there is a group of people who call themselves the Flat Earth Society. They claim the Bible backs up their belief. (It doesn't.) And they say some pilots claim they can't see any curvature to the earth. (I would say those pilots seriously need an eye exam.)

If the earth were flat, since light rays don't bend from passing through air, how could it be possible that there is a continuous sunrise and sunset moving across the earth? What kind of a defiant nature results in anyone supporting such an organization as the Flat Earth Society in this day and age?

Then I thought about all the overwhelming evidence that everything we see in nature has to be from intelligent design. The truth is out about the lies used to promote evolution; yet look at all the highly educated people who defiantly refuse to even consider the possibility of anything coming from a creator. Is their reasoning demented, or do they share a hatred of God with Satan?

There is one more concern I would like to clear up before continuing with this book. There are people of some beliefs that detest the testimony of the Holy Bible that the living God of the universe has a Son named Jesus Christ, who rose from the dead.

Some people, by their religious belief, feel it is their duty to kill you if you believe Jesus Christ of Nazareth in the Holy Bible to be God's Son. And some non-Christian people strictly forbid themselves and their relatives from studying any doctrines other than their own. However, with all the undisputable evidence being found in science, nature and historic archives, God might as well be saying, "Put me to the test and I will prove to you who I am," because he has.

Throughout the Old Testament, it explained that Jesus would be coming to earth to save us from our sinful nature, and it gave plenty of good reasons why that would be necessary to redeem us from our sins. Moses, a man other religions trust, talked about Jesus Christ coming to earth to save mankind from our sins. Some religions believe in angels but forbid any belief of Jesus Christ being God's Son. They say, there is no one (and nothing) on an equal with God Almighty.

Well, Jesus even said that. He said there is nothing He can do without the authority being given to Him by His Father, Jehovah, God Almighty. And God's title implies just that—almighty!

The Lord's Prayer states, "It shall be done on earth as it is in heaven." This means it took place in heaven first. That's why I can't understand anyone having difficulty believing that God has a Son, Jesus.

Let's look at this another way. Aren't there lots of fathers on earth who assign their sons as agents to look after their business? If this is customary on earth, why should anyone reject God enjoying the same personal relationship with a Son of His own?

Another thing I find very strange is that although many belief systems agree God can raise people from the dead, they refuse to believe God could have raised His own Son from the dead. This does not make reasonable sense to me.

Some demand proof of Jesus Christ's resurrection. Well, there are several ways you can look at this:

1. Historical archives by rulers who did not even know God and other educated people who lived in the time of Jesus wrote about him.

2. Before Christ's gruesome death on the cross, all His followers distanced themselves from being affiliated with Him in any way. However, after they witnessed His resurrection, they became incredibly bold preaching about it, seemingly unconcerned that this bold preaching was likely to result in them being gruesomely executed.

3. Several lawyers—Christian, atheist, and otherwise—have scrutinized the historical records and archives and concluded Jesus must have risen from the dead. They base their conclusion on the fact that those who said they witnessed the resurrected Son of God, Jesus Christ, refused to retract their statements even when under the threat of any kind of horrific death sentence that many suffered for not denying His resurrection. In fact, no history has been found where any of them denied that Christ had risen from the dead.

Based on these facts, I believe everything the New Testament of the Holy Bible says about Jesus Christ. Therefore, I hope you will not condemn me or this book for anything I mention in it about God's only begotten Son, Jesus Christ of Nazareth, or anything I mention about God's creation.

Defiance against the obvious truth is nothing new. It has been an ongoing repeated pattern for some who hate the truth that they know is true. I say this because now, sixty years or so after the Second World War, there are some who were not born until decades later who insist that the Holocaust, the killing of six million Jews, never happened. Why?

Well, there has been a lot of hatred for Jewish people down through time. I guess it is no surprise to hear some of these people now denying that the Holocaust ever happened. I find this no different than the evident history of Jesus Christ of Nazareth's time on earth being denied shortly afterward. Some seek for truth, and others seek to justify what they want to believe. However, *hating the truth does not change the truth.*

In seeking for the truth in every way available, I understand. I've come to believe the New Testament is about the time Jesus spent on earth. It is fact that He lived a perfect life without sinning, that He died an unjust death to redeem us from our sins, and that His Father, God Almighty, resurrected Him from the dead *because it was an unjust death.*

Knowing where we came from is vitally important to knowing what is best for us now and for our future. The most important history of where we came from is in the Holy Bible. That is what this book is all about.

How Lies Affect Our Sexuality

This chapter covers this topic as I experienced it in my life. The stories I'll relate here are dramatized true events. Please do not think I am embittered by these experiences; on the contrary, I feel fortunate to have been a part of them and to be able to share them as a way to illustrate some of the important points in this book. My hope is that these illustrations may help you to attain a better perception on how to live your life and get the most joy out of it.

During the first five years of my life, half of my time was spent in the hospital, terribly sick with nephritis, an inflammation of the kidneys that caused fluid to back up in my body.

Because of this sickness, over the years, I learned to endure and to accept responsibility for some hardships. I had to have medication needles poked into my backside daily. Also, I had to take bitter pills every day for years. Because I knew the sadness of living with constant pain, I also understood and felt sympathetic sadness when I saw other people suffering from sick-ness and handicapped situations.

Witnessing and being able to relate to their mis-ery caused me to mature early in life. I especially matured in the sense of sympathetically wanting to take responsible care of others. I do not know how to explain it best, but I would say I developed a strong desire to shelter myself and others from misfortune and pain.

In the early 1950s, the medical institutions' poli-cies of the day did not allow children to go into a hos-pital to visit the sick. This policy was believed to be in the best interest for healthy children, but it was a sad one; we could not visit or play with our siblings. I can vividly remember waving to my brothers from a sealed window five stories up.

Under these circumstances, I became determined to cooperate and to concentrate on whatever was necessary to get well. However, this was not the only experience of my early childhood that affected my outlook on life.

By the time I was four, the nurses let me roam around the hospital and visit people in the other wards. I found it interesting to visit the teenagers' ward, where I learned lots of swear words without understanding what they were. I had to be taught which words should not be used. Also, by the time I was about five or so, I learned some basic knowledge about how babies come to exist.

Sexual intercourse made far better sense than the dumb stories my grandmother told me about a stork. (When I asked my mother, she backed up my grandmother's story to avoid talking about sex.) Since then, the general ethics of communication between adults and youths has become more open and honest concerning the facts of life, but lots of problems still exist.

When I was about eight or nine, nothing had changed. My parents were still unwilling to be truthful with me about sex. I got ticked off from hearing lies about how children come to exist, and one day, I decided enough was enough. It was high time to set the facts straight.

It was Christmas Day. We were all seated at the table, and a conversation started about the difference between boys and girls. And once again, my grandmother said, "Girls are made of sugar and spice and everything nice. Boys are made of snakes and snails and puppy dog tails." I was disgusted with the lies.

I blurted out, "That's not true. I know the difference between boys and girls." I was about to say boys have penises and girls have vaginas. However, just then, my mother was walking into the dining room carrying the Christmas turkey on a platter. She had a startled look on her face—a look that told me she was about to drop it because of what she feared I might know and was about to say. Suddenly, I felt desperate to figure out a way to calm the deathly quiet tension in that room. And I solved it by resorting to a lie too. I said, "God took a rib from Adam to make Eve. Therefore, boys have one less rib than girls do."

The look of relief on my mother's face was like a death sentence had been waived in her favor. Yes, I had saved the turkey, but the uneasiness in our family whenever the topic of sex came up went on for many more years to come.

My parents separated when I was nine, and I did not want to upset my mother. So we never had a conversation about sex until I was in my mid-twenties, and even then, it wasn't talked about openly and honestly.

My mother raised us up to be honest, responsible, and morally decent citizens. She taught us to have respect for other people and be fair in our dealings with them. My father taught the same values when he was around. However, I did not get much in the way of sex education at home from either of them.

In the fifties and early sixties, sex was an embarrassing subject that caused many youths to shun away from talking to adults about it. This was a direct result of the immature and ashamed way children saw adults act regarding anything sexual. From the time we were old enough to understand simple conversation right up through our teens, those of us who overheard adults were all receiving the same signals from them. This wasn't healthy and some of it was nonsense with far-reaching effects. Some examples are the expressions and sounds we observed from adults when we touched our private parts or merely hugged another child of the opposite sex as we played—expressions which mockingly insinuated something sexual or sexually perverse was going on. Children mimicked this strange adult behavior when they figured a child in their presence had said or done anything that seemed affectionate toward a child of the opposite sex.

This immature and inappropriate behavior was common in most of the adults I grew up around. Even as children, we felt we were the object of *whisper talk* whenever someone might think we had developed affection for a person of the opposite sex. The impression I remember those actions having on me as a child was that adults considered what they were thinking about was too unethical to be put into understandable language. (Unfortunately, it's still all too common for raised eyebrows and drawn out "ooohs" and more to be meted out to anyone showing affection—from children to pensioners. The intentionally embarrassing gossipy nonsense exhibited by people of all ages about the beginnings of relationships by couples of all ages is absolutely ridiculous.) Another example is when I've mentioned the title of my book. Immediately most people gasp at hearing the word "sexual" mentioned in the title.

As another example of how unhealthy attitudes were toward sex back then, society considered it to be unorthodox for a husband to be in the delivery room with his wife when she was having a baby. Thank goodness for the protest put up against this. (In 1971, Margaret Trudeau refused to have her son born in the hospital unless her husband, Pierre Elliott Trudeau, could be there with her. Pierre Trudeau was, at this time, the prime minister of Canada. Margaret's well-publicized stand helped abolish the silly rules restricting husbands from being in delivery rooms for the births of their children. However, many generations passed down the "doctors only" attitude regarding sex and sexuality.)

Some attitudes have changed for the better since then, but other attitudes have become worse in that they have caused most children and young teenagers to still regard sex in a very immature manner and as something to be ashamed of. This mentality expressed in adults erodes attitudes of positive self-esteem in children when they learn the truth about how they came to be and sometimes can cause irreversible damage for life.

The Destructive Power of Lies

I had a very sad experience when I was twelve years old. It was related to shame around the subject of sex. It started one day in the spring of 1962. I was on my way to school when I met a student who was new in the neighborhood. He was the same age, height, and build as I was and went to the same school. We talked about the different activities to do around town for fun. Then we started talking about the girls in the school. I said that I believed that one girl in our school was very foxy. He wasn't familiar with the term, and I explained that *foxy* meant a girl looked sexy or attractive, and that she wanted to look that way to members of the male sex. However, this student stopped dead in his tracks and stared at me with a puzzled look on his face.

I said, "Don't you know about sex?"

"No," he said, looking even more puzzled.

Without considering how he would take what I blurted out, I told him in a couple of quick sentences what his father and mother did to make him.

He glared at me and said, "My dad didn't do that to my mother."

I said, "I'm not lying to you, man. That's just the facts of life. Ask anybody around here. Ask your father."

He said he would and stomped off to his class.

I didn't think anything more about our talk until I greeted him on the way to school the next day and asked him if he had talked to his dad.

He said, "Yes I did," in a disturbed voice. "My father told me that what you told me was an utter lie, and that if I wanted to do a good service for the Lord, I should beat the hell out of you because you are a demon to have told me that."

I was stunned. "Did your dad really say that?"

He said, "Yes, he did." Then he lifted his fists. "You have to throw the first punch because you're the bad guy."

I have never liked fighting, and I certainly did not want to fight someone I liked. Since he was determined that only a bad guy would throw the first punch, no fight got started. However, after four days of trying to get me to hit him, he got so frustrated with not being able to follow his father's instructions that he accidentally slugged me.

Although I had been trying for days to convince him that babies really are conceived through sexual intercourse, his dad had brainwashed him so badly that he refused to hear what I had to say, and he would not listen to others who were circling us to see a fight.

That student was an intelligent loyal son to his father, and I really admired that about him. Unfortunately, his dad was a very strict fanatic about moral conduct. So much so that he had lost touch with reality and told a desperate lie about sex to his twelve-year-old son to hide what could not be hidden.

Anyway, the fight finally started, and it ended when I got him in a painful hold and he gave up. The next day, I got called into the office to get the strap for fighting in the school zone. But it didn't end there. The boy's father told the principal that I had beat up his son. That made me angry for the first time over this whole incident. I told the principal what happened and how much I regretted all of it. He shook my hand while thanking me for telling him the truth. Then the principal called the student's father into the school to try to give him some sensible advice. However, that did not work.

Shortly afterward, the student's family moved out of the neighborhood. Then something odd happened. About six months later, they moved back into the same house. And to my surprise, I found out that the boy was *still* intent on fighting me! He was still convinced that I told him a lie; he still had not learned anything about sex. And his dad was still telling him lies and instructing his son, who was now becoming a teenager, to "do a good service for the Lord" by beating the devil out of me.

It did not take him long to find me, and when he did, there were lots of other young boys around; we were out tobogganing. Once again, I pleaded with him to ask any one of them about sex; and once again, he refused to, insisting instead that I start a fight with him again. Finally, I walked away. He resorted to calling me a "chicken shit nigger baby." At this point, I decided if he wanted a fight that bad, I would oblige him—and this time, I started it.

The biggest problem with that fight was that neither of us were scrappers, and neither of us had a vicious desire to hurt the other. Neither one of us had a hostile temper. As soon as I had hit him once, the anger I had felt for what he said to me was gone. My thoughts went back to wondering about the stupid reasoning behind why we were fighting. I was dumbfounded as to why, after six months, that young man had not learned anything about sex. While I was thinking about the pathetic insanity that caused the fight to get started instead of concentrating on the fact that I was in one, he began to get the upper hand. Eventually though, I got him into the same hold I had got him into before, and he once again said, "I give up." I had released him and started walking away when I got hit from behind. That, along with all the rest of the ignorance, finally caused me to flip out. He got hurt this time.

As I left to go home, a friend pointed out the boy's father, who was standing at the top of the hill, and told me he had cheered his son on while it looked like he was winning. I was angry again. If there is anything I can't stand, it is a religious hypocrite, and now I was glaring at one. I won't describe the hate I felt for that man at that time. He caused me to hurt his son, a boy I liked and felt very sorry for.

The family moved out of the neighborhood again. I saw the boy a couple of years later and he had, of course, finally learned about sex. He told me he had left home at age fourteen, and that he hated his father for what he had done to him. We shared regrets and apologies over what had happened between us. However, what still bothered me was: Why on earth had it happened in the first place? What possessed that boy's father to tell his son such outrageous lies? It didn't make any sense. I could not help believing that his father sincerely loved his children. He appeared to be a decent respectable man with a good education, and he was a good provider for his family. What deep-rooted problem caused this sad ending between a father and his son?

What I learned from this was that, as parents, we must try to guard ourselves against becoming deceiving hypocrites in our children's eyes about anything; otherwise, we may permanently lose respect from them to some degree. We must do our best to be real and honest, use integrity, and never give advice that we know is a lie. We cannot turn our backs on them or tell them mythical fairy tales instead of the truth to avoid talking about sex or any other subject.

How Lies Affect Trust

Typical examples of fairy-tale lies are Santa Claus and the Easter Bunny. Trying to convince children to believe in such lies can lead to future humiliation for them. I still remember the embarrassment I felt when I realized later why other students had laughed at me and teased me for believing in Santa Claus.

My parents had provided false evidence for us to find, so we would believe that Santa had come to our house. One Christmas Eve, I woke up hearing footsteps crunching in the snow on the roof over my head and bells jingling. Then the footsteps stopped, and the bells sounded as if they went off into the distance rapidly. I jumped out of bed and ran to the living room. Under the tree was a big pile of presents, even though my parents were so poor that they were scrounging all the time to make ends meet. And even more convincing was the snow on the floor.

And one rainy Easter Sunday, my brothers and I found big muddy footprints going through our house. The footprints had a hopping pattern like that of a rabbit; however, we had no pets.

Trusting the evidence I'd seen with my own eyes and blindly believing adults I'd placed my trust in, I argued with my peers that these fictitious beings with supernatural abilities were real just like God and Jesus Christ. At that time, I did not have any proof that *they* existed and had performed miracles either, but because of my trust in my elders, I was firm in my belief that they did.

And there were lots of other mysterious things around, like the television set which showed amazing cartoon characters. I had no knowledge of how animated cartoons were made. As a young child, I had no reason to doubt the cartoons were just as real as Santa Claus and God.

My parents had gone to a lot of trouble to convince us that Santa Claus existed and they were successful. What other children thought of my belief did not bother me as long as I believed, but almost a year after I'd heard the footsteps and the sleigh bells, my brothers and I found hidden presents—presents that ended up under the tree on the night of December 24th.

When I discovered that there is no such thing as Santa Claus, I started to wonder if God and Jesus Christ were also lies. After all, people associated Christmas with them too. And of course I sure felt stupid, especially as I wondered what the students I went to school with thought of me for having believed in Santa Claus.

Can you imagine being fourteen, like my young friend, and learning that you have been tricked into fighting with your fellow student who actually told you the truth about sex? What an embarrassment that would be. What trust would we have left for any parent who lied to us like that? How could a father do that to his son?

I suppose it is quite simple to understand when we look at the brainwashing history that has affected us all. The history that we have inherited from our ancestors has taught us to accept mythical lies of every sort, and everyone follows the leader. So, if the government and religious leaders of the world exchange the truth for lies all the time, then why wouldn't their followers continue doing the same with their children? After all, theirs is the example from which we have learned. But what type of a leader are we if we teach our followers that the truth is a lie and convince them to believe that a pack of lies is the truth? How can we believe in these leaders anymore when we find out that they have deliberately misled us? How can anyone trust or have confidence in their support on anything after that?

As trusting followers, trying to make sense out of confusing lies, we ask our religious leaders difficult questions. To pacify their followers, the leaders cover up lies with more lies, eventually telling so many confusing lies that their congregation gets tired of asking for clarification.

When things get too far out of hand, the religious leaders may tell their more inquisitive members that the answers to their questions are "holy mysteries" or "holy secrets," that we should trust them without question, and their humble followers blindly obey. As a result, we have had centuries of compounded mythical lies and magic hocus-pocus taught to anyone trusting enough to believe and brainwashed to support the cult's self-serving motives. Once we learn we should not have trusted, we begin to question our ability to see who is behaving deceitfully. We question whether or not we can trust the people closer to us.

Surely the young man who had been deceived by his father must have struggled to trust anyone, even those closest to him.

Traits of the Habitual Liar

I have often noticed that when people are telling a story that is a lie, getting deeper into their exaggerations, a certain delight comes over them. When they are asked what truth there is to their story, they get tense and defensive, often telling more lies in order to conceal the truth. If they're successful, the gullible audience doubts the truth and trusts in the lies. However, if the storyteller fails to convince the listeners, then it is only with great reluctance that the liar admits the truth.

This is the *opposite* of the way that they should feel about the lies they have created. Telling the truth should be a joy, and to feel the need to tell a lie should be an unwelcome misery. But the only lying that causes the tale-teller to feel uneasy is the impromptu lie to cover up a former lie, and this is rather like breaking new ground with a plow. It is tough, but if the added lie appeases their audience, then it becomes a delight to repeat it the next time. (This became very evident with the father of my young friend. He became obsessed with his lies, compounding them as his son believed what he was saying.)

It seems strange that people would tell such stories, but consider what kind of stories most people prefer to read. The clear majority prefer fiction over nonfiction. To capture interest, tall tales tickle the ears of most listeners; most audiences are already primed to embrace lies. But we should never be closed-minded about finding out for ourselves what the truth *really* is. This is especially important when you find out there are several beliefs or opinions about a subject. Although my young friend had plenty of opportunity to ask others around us for the truth about sex, he was too loyal to his father; he refused to risk shaking his faith in his dad.

The Perils of Blind Faith

Many people adopt a faith or belief system, be it some Christian faith like Baptist, Catholic, Jehovah's Witness, Buddhism, Islam, Atheism, or even evolutionist beliefs and then close their minds to the possibilities that any other belief may be right. Often, whatever faith the individual was first exposed to was so impressive that they close their minds to the need to look any further to find out for sure what the truth really is. No cross examination or critical thought is applied.

Through time, deceitful lies have been brainwashed into all of us until we learn the truth about them—if we ever do. Oddly enough, even after people learn the truth, they often continue to automatically follow the old deceitful patterns. When a child loses a tooth, the parent recommends putting it under their pillow so the tooth fairy will exchange it for money. Parents say such things as automatically as breathing, knowing full well that it is a complete lie.

This is, unfortunately, a deep-rooted custom. It is so deeply rooted that simple and ordinary parents have rigidly adopted it as a training pattern for their offspring for thousands of years. It is a brainwashing tradition that all of society needs to recognize and decide to put an end to. One of the Ten Commandments states, "Thou shalt not lie." That means no lying about anything. Period.

In Matthew 5:19–20, Jesus spoke about what happens when people teach and believe in mythical lies from unrighteous leaders,

> Whosoever, therefore shall break one of these least commandments, and shall teach men so, he shall be called the least in the kingdom of heaven: but whosoever shall do and teach them, the same shall be called great in the kingdom of heaven.
>
> For I say unto you, That except your righteousness shall exceed the righteousness of the scribes and the Pharisees, you shall in no case enter into the kingdom of heaven.

To tell a false story seems to not be nearly as serious a crime as murdering someone. Yet Jesus said, "Whosoever, therefore, shall break one of these least commandments [for example, lies] and shall teach men so, he shall be called the least in the kingdom of heaven." This shows that the practicing of a false mythical pagan ritual is a curse, affecting not only those who teach it but also those who adopt it as a part of their custom. This is especially true if, even after they know full well that it is false, they keep on practicing it, as is done in many Christian religions.

This sort of pagan ritual is embraced by many other non-Christian faiths too. And basically, nobody seems to feel the least bit uneasy about these practices because they have been passed down for many centuries of ancestors.

The Bible explains just how badly cursed anyone is who either teaches or desires to dwell on mythical falsehood customs. In Exodus 34:6–7, God declared to Moses the effect that such practices would have. There it says,

> And the LORD passed by before
> him, and proclaimed, The LORD God,
> merciful and gracious, longsuffering,
> and abundant in goodness and truth,
> Keeping mercy for thousands,
> forgiving iniquity and transgression
> and sin, and that will by no means
> clear the guilty; visiting the iniquity
> of the fathers upon the children,

and upon the children's children, unto the third and to the fourth generation.

Summarizing the meaning of these two verses, God will forgive us of any unrighteous evil that we may have done *if we quit it when we learn better*. However, if anyone knows full well that what they are doing and teaching is wrong but persist in practicing it, they are guilty. Therefore, if any of us as a parent teaches falsehood to our children, we not only curse ourselves, we also curse our offspring.

I have seen this firsthand from many students I knew in high school. The sheltered life they had lived because of the spoiling they got from their parents, who failed to teach them the harsh realities in life, caused them to go from living in a fairy-tale life to reality in a very short time, a reality for which they were not equipped.

Youths need all the truthful support they can get on sexuality and any other subject they may be confronted with. The time to start being truthful with them is from the time they are born. Then it will be easier for us as parents to deal with the truth later in life when we are confronted with difficult realities we must explain. If we always tell the truth, our children will develop a strong trusting bond with us; they know their parents have always provided them with the plain truth and were never closed-minded hypocrites. Always teach the truth about all subjects to the best of your ability.

The plain truth prevents psychological frustration. Many teenagers go through shock when they suddenly find themselves confronted with the plain truth about reality. Suddenly, concerned that they do not know who they really are any more say, "They need to find themselves." For many of the students I went to school with, the lost sense of security was frightening. I believe this happened because after listening to so many fairy tales and being sheltered by their parents from reality for so long, they became disheartened and lost when faced with the realities of life.

Paradise Lost: Perils of a Fairy-Tale Childhood

Children can hear, "happily ever after" so often that it becomes an idealized belief. When children reach their teen years believing that something of a mystical nature will keep them safe, reality comes as a devastating shock. Often, this causes them to turn to an escape, like drugs, an all-too-convenient false crutch for youths who are trying to determine the difference between reality and mythical fiction after hearing too many lies for so many years.

The custom of sheltering children from reality for so many generations causes parents to feel pressured to follow suit. If a parent prefers to be honest with their children about Santa Claus, the Easter Bunny, the tooth fairy, etc., they face a great deal of pressure from other adults. For example, your child loses one of their baby teeth, and other adults are already telling your child to put their tooth under their pillow so the tooth fairy will exchange it for money. As your child's eyes become bright with the anticipation, you find yourself biting your tongue to avoid making a scene, and your silence confirms what the other adults have said is true.

These customs are extremely tough to break away from, especially if your spouse also talks to your children as though these mythical characters really exist. But the eventual truth comes as a shock and can leave us lost. When we are faced with indisputable facts that contradict our understanding of reality, many frightening questions can arise. And when the adults we have trusted are the ones who taught us the falsehoods, we suddenly find ourselves all alone and confused, not knowing who we can trust.

In early childhood, our children are particularly vulnerable to any type of a lie taught to them as the truth by the adults they love and trust. When I learned, at the age of eight, that all my adult relatives had been lying to me for years about Santa Claus, I really became concerned as to whether Almighty God and Jesus Christ were frauds too. These new doubts eventually became very discomforting. At one point, the questions I was asking myself caused me to become hysterical with fear. If God in heaven who was supposed to have created us was a fake, then what made man, the earth, and the universe?

As I went from believing in resurrection to believing death would be for eternity, I thought about the frozen ground in the graveyard where my grandfather who had lived with us for years had recently been buried. I loved him and missed him so much, and now a horrifying fear of dying came over me: I would never get to see my grandfather again! I feared that he was forever lost, buried in that frozen ground out in the cemetery.

Although I was only eight years old, the mysterious comforts that I relied on were overshadowed by doubts on every account. I became terrified imagining what might actually be the truth regarding existence as I understood it and started having nightmares. I felt I could trust no one, felt skeptical about confiding in anyone to learn the truth. And I dreaded what the truth might be.

Questions flashed through my young mind. Am I being tested? Is everything I see just a fake? Why am I here? Am I all alone on this earth with robots that I have believed were my mother, father, brothers, neighbors, and so on?

We are not born with any depth of understanding about the technology to make a television set, but it is right before our eyes for us to believe in, and, of course, some of these thoughts came from watching television shows about space and robots. But some of these thoughts also arose from something I had witnessed but did not understand.

My brothers and I were playing with some kids from our neighborhood. We got tired of playing tag and were standing in a group, talking about whatever came into our young minds. One little girl was listening with the rest of us to a boy talking about what he and his dad did. When suddenly, a boy standing next to her turned, raised his fist, and punched her hard in the side of her head. She started to cry and rubbed the side of her head. I glared at the boy who hit her, wondering what kind of person could do a thing like that.

But I saw no sign of any remorse; he actually seemed to feel *good* about what he had done.

It was a very frightening incident because it was not logical. The boy, larger than the rest of us, was behaving like a machine. Machines operate without concern or understanding for the functions they exercise; if a mechanical device is set up to perform a certain function at a certain time, it will do it regardless of the circumstances. If your arm is in the way, it could be cut off or crushed. The cold and callous indifference of the boy who hit the little girl was, I thought, typical of what I would expect only a robot would do. Then I thought, *Has everything and everyone I have seen been part of an experiment or being used to test me?*

None of us can physically experience being anyone else's spirit. With my limited understanding, I questioned the reality of everything after learning Santa Claus was a fabricated lie; I wondered if I was the only living person on earth or if anything I had reasoned up to that time in my life was true because now I had no foundation to base anything on.

For me, the shock of feeling lost came early in life because I was always concerned about dealing with facts. I ended up detesting the mythical lies that had been entrenched in me by adults. I remember feeling nauseous just from listening to my teachers and other adults repeating the same mythical lies, and I looked at life with a lot more serious concern than an average child. This made it easier for me to adjust later as a teenager, accepting the realities as I learned about them.

Some young people grow up believing that love and marriage will protect them from problems in life. These people are living in the fairy-tale world of happily ever after. It's a statement they hear so often that it can become a hallucinating chant they trust in as a belief until reality hits. Eventually, they realize that they alone will have to be responsible for themselves against life's challenges. This can be extremely terrifying if you have been sheltered from the truths about reality.

About a month or so before graduation, I overheard a group of girls from well-to-do families talking about living on their own after completing school. One said she was going to find a rich guy to marry so he would look after her. She even mentioned getting pregnant first to snare him, if required. I was shocked to see her friends nodding their heads in agreement that this was a good idea. How desperately insecure those young ladies must have been, believing so strongly in the myth of happily ever after.

People placing their confidence in this type of strategy are setting themselves up for disaster. Forced to finally face reality, people who have engaged in this type of befuddled mythical reasoning often sink into depression, complaining of life being unfair toward them. The longer anyone harps on the unfairness of life to avoid maturing and accepting reality, the more paranoid they can become. And if they harden their hearts against accepting reality enough, I've found they can become schizophrenic. Schizophrenia is psychosis marked by withdrawn bizarre and sometimes delusional behavior and by intellectual and emotional deterioration.

Of the schizophrenic patients in psychiatric care, 95 percent of them are diagnosed between the ages of seventeen to twenty-four years old. It's the time when they are leaving high school, college, or university and the security of their parents' sheltering environment to make a life of their own. When expectations fail and they have not learned to deal with reality maturely, they become vulnerable victims to psychiatric drug dependency.

Some doctors of psychiatry say that schizophrenia is the result of a chemical imbalance in the brain. Based on my experiences and observations, I believe schizophrenia is the result of training a child to base reality on mythical lies. If chemical imbalance is a factor, I suspect it is developed from distorted reasoning, resulting from a person basing their logic on myth rather than reality. In my opinion, psychiatry is nothing more than a pill-pushing source of shut-up drugs that desensitize people to reality.

I say this because all the people I have known who ended up on these drugs became like vegetables, destroyed for life. Most of them were well-educated and alert people before being put on the drugs. After getting on them, they became aimless zombies. Reading the negative side effects of these drugs, it is little wonder.

Proverbs 26:29 describes the shocking truth of what parents and other people who prefer to embrace teaching mythical lies to children are doing:

A lying tongue hates those that are afflicted by it and a flattering mouth works ruin.

The clear majority of parents believe they absolutely and unequivocally love their children. But in reality, when you teach with lies, you are supporting Satan's intent to curse them.

What I believe all children need is wisdom counseling from an old sage. However, old sages are becoming very hard to find.

Many young people end up disappointed with life because of lies they learned to believe in from their parents. The boy I talked about earlier who had been lied to about sex was off to a new start with reality at the age of fourteen. However, how long would those high school girls be living in a dream world, probably raising their children to believe in the same mythical lies? How often do young girls get pregnant to secure a relationship only to find themselves dumped after being used? How many young men become husbands or fathers without having learned any more about responsibility and reality than the young women had? With parents raised to accept mythical doctrine as customary and entrench it in their children, it becomes a fixed curse to continue down through the generations. And for centuries, mankind has been substituting lies for the truth to avoid talking about sex.

Some people who are regarded as experts claim that mythical stories are good for children because they protect them from having to deal with the harsh realities of life while they are young. I disagree. I believe that these lies are only harmful to their stability and always have a negative impact on them to some degree when they eventually learn about reality.

The Bible tells us, often, that lies are the worst form of evil. This is because spiritual lies are the foundation leading to all other forms of physical evil and wickedness. Cheating, stealing, sexual misconduct, and even hating and murder are not as bad as lying since lying must come first, paving the way for the evil physical acts. Truth comes from a spirit that leads to all forms of righteousness. Lies come from a spirit that leads to all forms of unrighteousness. The destructive power of lies is so strongly saturated into society that without God's help, there would be no hope for any of us.

Seeking Solutions

Sex is a subject that nobody knows all the answers to. If your children ask questions you can't answer, seek counseling *together*. Read up on it, or seek advice from professionals. Working together to find answers could be an experience that will gain you more respect from your children and remove generational barriers. It is an opportunity to establish a more open and honest relationship with your child.

Children appreciate being treated with respect and truthfulness. They do not have to be lied to as though they are incapable of dealing with the truth. In short, lying to a child about sex or promoting any other lie is not protection for them. It only causes destruction of their confidence in life and diminishes their respect for their parents or guardians. Period.

Some people who don't know where the future is headed feel so hopelessly lost for a solution that could make life worth living; they come to believe that suicide is the only hope left for them to successfully find peace or at least end the misery that they are in.

The Bible foretold of the psychiatric depression that people are going through at this time, especially if they take a narrow view of life's purpose. The good news is the Holy Bible communicates to us what is righteousness and how to live and encourages teaching it to others. We can become aware of our promised Savior, Jesus Christ. Also, it teaches that by having faith in the righteousness of the Holy Bible rather than mythical pagan rituals of Babylon, we will have good reason to be happy about our lives.

Examine Your Faith

This is something you should explore for yourself to get the best benefit rather than listening to someone dictating what the Holy Bible (or any other religion or other doctrine) is about. If you don't bother to put your own personal effort into knowing it but rather rely solely on someone else teaching it to you, then you are lost. Regardless of how righteous and good a preacher may seem to be, the Holy Bible says, "Cursed be a man that trust in man and makes flesh his arm"(Jeremiah 17:5). It is good to seek counsel with others, but it is not good to blindly follow them. If you do not cross-examine the religions and their scriptures for yourself, you are not doing what Almighty God's word in the Holy Bible tells us to do for our own personal safety.

That Word says, "Give a portion to seven and also to eight; for we know not what evil shall be upon the earth" (Ecclesiastes 11:2). Seven is a complete number in the Bible, but it tells you to go beyond that. To me, this suggests that when you think you have found the answers, do not stop there. Keep on learning about righteousness and cross examine what you think you know. Do not let anybody blind you because although all of us are partly in the right, all of us are in the wrong to some extent. This is because not one of us is perfect. None of us are God.

The more we vow to live our lives with righteousness and truth, the less we will be plagued with the mythical lies and madness of pagan rituals that can burn us out. If you are wondering what can be done to correct this problem, then hopefully you have some of that answer in your hands because that's what this book is all about. I am not talking about the old ostrich trick of believing nobody can see you if you bury your head in the sand, pretending that everything is okay when it isn't. What I am talking about is the wisdom to cope with and survive the evils that are upon the earth without embracing them. I am talking about a happiness that is of good, a happiness that can be enjoyed even with the earth being as corrupt as it is.

Much of my understanding of many of the peculiar aspects of man has come from studying the Book of Proverbs. It was written by Solomon, King of Israel in the tenth century BC. History describes King Solomon as the wisest man who ever lived. I believe he must have been because his rule supported the longest known historical period of world peace. Therefore, I have related observations that I have made of mankind to the many rules of behavior that are written in Proverbs. Also, I have read other books, scriptural, and otherwise about man's conscious and subconscious characteristics. The understanding that I have found has made life for me well worthwhile.

Studying, pondering personal experiences, and discussing thoughts on the subjects of life with other people have, together, produced a lot of peace in my life. Even when I have had to endure very trying times, I have found confidence through the experiences, faith, and understanding I have in the laws of wisdom I found in the Holy Bible. This has helped me to learn even more on the most probable reasons why people really think and act the way they do in connection with various aspects about themselves and others. I even went to college to study this subject because it has been a personal interest of mine to understand why everything is as it is without being prejudiced in comparing one belief against another one.

At a friend's advice, to improve my writing skills, I began a humanities course, an entrance course for university. The professor had us read and write reports on the mythical gods of Greece. I kept making conflicting comparison arguments in my reports using biblical quotes. The professor became increasingly annoyed at me for mentioning anything to do with the Holy Bible, and I dropped out of the course, thoroughly convinced that what my dad told me when I was eight years old was absolutely correct. At that time, he was telling me about his experience in talking to university students who were travelling on the trains he worked on back in the forties and fifties as a porter. They all seemed to believe that the wisdom they were learning from their university training was far more valuable than what they could learn from the Bible.

They also stated that they absolutely did not believe there was a creator of the universe. Dad told me he believed "university is a place to bleach out any common sense that might have been left in a person after they finish high school." He believed that if you refused to accept and share their lie that there is no God of the Holy Bible, then you would not make it through university. That was exactly what I experienced in my arguments with my humanities professor.

My dad believed that for anyone to gain any worthwhile wisdom, they had to study the Word of God in the Holy Bible and compare it to what we find in nature. I relied on my dad's wise advice to learn about my interest on why people behave the way most of them do. The most guarded value I believe people have of their own sexuality and the views they have for other people's sexuality is expressed to some extent in almost everything anyone says and does. This is because there is almost nothing a person can talk about or react to that does not reveal something about their most deep-seated feeling on the subject. If you are wondering how this is possible, then consider the law that says, "From the heart the mouth speaketh" (Matthew 12:34). Spend some time over the next few days, after you have talked to someone, thinking back now and then about what you have just said. Consider this:

- Why did I say what I just said?
- Why did I say it the way I said it?
- What type of a feeling did I have while I was saying what I said?
- Did I exaggerate on anything even just a little bit? If I did, why did I?

It doesn't matter whether you try to guard what you say or not, the biblical law, "From the heart the mouth speaketh" will hold true every time.

If you want to tell the truth, then you will because that will be your deepest concern. If you do not want to tell the truth, then you will not tell the truth. And if you feel that you want to tell the truth but when you speak, an exaggeration that is a lie comes out, then your true faith will have been in lying. That faith, which comes from your heart, wins out. And often this comes from a desire to fascinate. We think it will make a more interesting story; we want to control what the listener believes about us. Why? Is it an ego trip? Or is it because as a child, we experienced the thrill of exaggerated mythical lies, and we hunger to tell stories with the same amount of zeal?

It is amazing how something can become a part of you, and you do not even realize this has happened. After giving this some thought, don't you agree about how subtly such influences to exaggerate can influence us?

The feelings in your heart (love and concern for yourself and others, charity, jealous resentment, love or hatred for barbaric attitudes) can all be examined by the way you talk about almost anything. What you may think of as a lighthearted joke often has a strong bearing on what your real values are, and these values usually originate from what you learned from your parents. This has affected the natural good quality of our human sexuality that our Creator originally blessed us with, from our childhood right up to our old age.

The morality of sexuality is one of the most controversial aspects of everyone's life. It is the major subject in the Holy Bible too. It teaches what is good for you (how to enjoy the happiest sexual enjoyment in your life) and explains the consequences of indulging in sexual activity that is bad for you.

Some religions have twisted the truth of the Holy Bible and replaced it with blind faith lies. The lies they use have promoted sexual immorality such as polygamy cults, hate groups such as the Ku Klux Klan and ISIS, plus other forms of ignorance, resulting in confusion and wars. Some lies have been made up by religious leaders to intentionally promote hatred for the Creator of the universe, God Almighty.

The New Testament gives all kinds of warnings about deceitful preachers making out like they are God or Jesus Christ Himself for their own personal manipulating intentions. This evil insanity has helped some of their collection plates to become overloaded with money. To achieve this, some preach terrifying punishment to those who do not support the faith financially. Some who call themselves God-fearing leaders have twisted the truth to promote public support for their own immoral lusts and even used religion to insist these practices were for leaders only, and everyone else would be condemned for doing the same.

In one immoral practice from the Dark Ages, some churches required a young couple who were in love with each other to allow the commander of the faith to go to bed with the bride first. They acted as though they were God Himself blessing their marriage by engaging in sexual intercourse with the virgin wife before the groom touched her. Not surprisingly, some people no longer wanted to be married by the church.

The motives behind this kind of corrupt cultish behavior was (and still is) to brainwash followers through fear into total subservience. This gives the organization financial power and the power to use the women and children as the leaders' submissive sex slaves.

Some cults made strict laws to maintain control. One such law made it illegal for people to study the Holy Bible; to enforce it, anyone caught with a Holy Bible in their possession was burned at the stake in the town square as an example. In this way, they could keep the common people ignorant of their righteous rights.

As God's children, we need not consider ourselves subject to bondage by any man. Period. We are offered the right of our own free will to honor our loving Father in heaven—or not. The Holy Bible clearly explains this in so many ways throughout the Old and especially the New Testament.

Through education, some people are starting to wake up to the corruption of cults and their ways. They are learning about the precious love God Almighty has for us all. The more these people are learning about how badly they have been lied to, the hungrier they are getting for the truth.

Others whose pride causes them to be defiant against any responsible laws of righteousness embrace and practice demonic cult ways. They honor the unrighteous laws that support corrupt business strategies, immoral sex, adultery, easy divorces, and abortion as their justified personal rights in defiance of God Almighty's responsible loving ways. They refuse to accept there being any authority higher than themselves by embracing the proven falsehood of evolution. They even proclaim that they are their own god.

What good are we to anyone when we exchange the truth in any way for mythical falsehoods? Man's history is saturated with the practice of mythological lies to mesmerize and exploit people.

Beware the Power of Salesmanship

While waiting for service on my car one day, I was wandering around the dealership's showroom. I noticed a small sign in one of the sales offices: "A good salesman is someone who can tell you to go to hell in such a way that you will be looking forward to the trip." Cults use this type of salesmanship to brainwash their followers. The only way to protect yourself from this is to read the Holy Bible yourself and pray for Jehovah God Almighty's help in understanding its teachings.

Be clean, loving, and truthful in spirit, soul, and body—as our Lord and Savior, Jesus Christ, lovingly advised—to get the best joy out of life.

Why Is Sex Considered Dirty?

Many people consider sex as dirty due to its common association with organs that remove waste substance from our bodies. Although these organs get little respect, the functions they perform are vital to a healthy body, just as the contributions of those who perform domestic cleaning chores are vital to a healthy environment.

Making demeaning jokes about the natural functions of our bodies' waste removal systems is the first step to building up a negative mental attitude toward them. For ages, our society downplayed the worthiness of the penis, vagina, breast, and anus, all essential organs of the human body. Man has done this so much that he has resorted to approval of widespread demoralizing exhibitions of the human anatomy's private parts for degenerate entertainment. It is like a public execution, thrusting mortal wounds at the worth of our body's waste removal and related sexual organ systems. The very source of man's existence is the part of him that he perverts the most.

Man slanders himself when he speaks degradingly about body organs. Typical examples of this are when someone addresses someone else by calling them a slang word for the rectum, penis, or vagina. When anyone talks like this, they are cursing the source of their own existence. Why is it that man associates his body's hygiene organs and his Creator with anything he might hate? Where did the influence to belittle the source of man's fertility come from in the first place?

We instinctively know the ever-increasing promotion of immoral sex is neither right nor justifiable, but society keeps on promoting it. This has caused parents to cast shame on sexuality as a part of life, and they lie to their children about sex, and they lie about reality. This does nothing good for children. It does not benefit them with a carefree life of bliss in their youth. What it does is leave them unprepared to object to immoral influences to which they will certainly be exposed.

Speak with respect were respect is due. Do not engage in or listen to conversation that degrades the waste removal or sexual parts (or any other parts) of our bodies. The need for children to learn honesty, trust, and decent respect for their sexuality from their parents is crucially important. The lack of it can leave very ugly ideas in a child's mind about their sex organs. If they first learn all the immoral attitudes associated with sex that are promoted on the street, it becomes a curse to them that you have not taught them otherwise. As we all know, first impressions are the most lasting. Therefore, prevent injury to your children by first being morally decent yourself. If you are in the habit of cussing and swearing, stop it dead now. If this means you have to learn a new vocabulary, do it. It will be one of the best gifts you can give to yourself, and bless everyone around you with respectable speech, especially your children. Let it be well known by the way you talk about the private parts of your body that you highly respect them as a blessing to our lives.

Shared Responsibility

One way to promote your respect for the waste removal systems of your body is for you to show it is as much Dad's job to change a baby's diaper as it is Mom's. If there are no babies left as an example for the older ones to witness, let them know that you both made it your business to make sure they were changed with a high regard for doing the job properly so they did not have to suffer from diaper rash or any other illness.

Some men scoff at the thought of changing a dirty diaper yet claim that they love the son or daughter who needs a diaper change to protect their health. How much do these men really love their children and their wife? God did not make man to dominate over women or to be dominated by women but rather to be equal partners as helpmates for each other. Genuinely loving fathers feel no shame in letting other men know they have no reluctance about changing a baby's diaper. Everyone loves the joy of hearing a baby laughing and smiling with that look of love in their eyes for you. Everyone should have the same amount of loving desire to share in doing everything they can to protect babies from becoming sad neglected individuals.

The experience lived by children in their first few years plays a big part in how they become as adults. Therefore, love them from the time they are first conceived, unconditionally, so hopefully they will grow up with the same loving ways.

Toiletry and Hygiene

If you have not read the previous chapters in this book, then please do read all of them before reading this one. Otherwise, the significant importance and respect that should be given to some of the subject matter will be missed.

Doing your toiletry tasks each morning should be done with the same zeal that you would have in getting ready for a first-time date. You want your date to be impressed and find you irresistibly alluring. And to do the job right requires far more than a clean face, combed hair, and brushed teeth. How about under your clothes, inside your body, and your mind? When your attitude is to be thoroughly clean, and you know you're thoroughly clean, then that aspect will radiate from you.

Do you smell of any undesirable odors such as stale perspiration, urine seepage, or a smear of feces from expelled gastric gases? A quick two-minute shower from time to time would be all that you need. It is an especially good idea to do this on hot days.

Soap chemicals should not be required every time you shower unless you have bad water where you live. A quick rinse using your hands or a terry cloth to scrub your skin, especially in high odor areas, is sometimes all you need. This will keep the stale perspiration of decaying cells under control without stripping your skin's natural oils. This oil is important protection against disease and infections. When it has been stripped off (especially if the soap is not being properly rinsed off in areas where your skin lies against other parts of itself), rashes and bacteria can invade your skin. This is a common problem in the armpits and pubic area, causing a painful skin irritation that stimulates an impulse to scratch. Scratching can rapidly intensify the damage done to your skin, causing you to run to the pharmacist or doctor for expensive medical treatments. It is a lot cheaper to use water and to rinse off thoroughly when you use soap products that alter the pH balance of your skin.

Another reason you should want to protect your skin's natural oil is that it gives off the stimulating sexual scent of your male or female body. Scrub off the bad odor that smothers the good odor.

Sometimes during hot weather, you may need to shower away from home. However, you may not have a change of underwear to put on. If this happens, take your underwear in the shower with you, wash, and rinse it out. Then wring it out, cover it in a dry towel, and wring it out again. This will make your underwear dry enough to wear it again. Also, when you put your underwear back on, it will feel refreshingly cool for a longer period of time on hot days. This is from the refrigeration effect of evaporation taking place in the material.

Men should make it a habit to sit on a toilet just like women do to urinate. Do not be a dog voiding all over the toilet. Have respect for females who need to sit on it. Some stubborn men argue that they always lift the seat before urinating in a toilet from a standing position. However, that is not good enough. The backsplash from this practice gets all over the toilet rim. Some backsplash also gets on the floor that makes it stink like a sewer. No matter how careful you think you might be at urinating into a toilet from a standing position, it is not good enough. Be considerate and have respect for whoever has the job of cleaning the toilet and the floor around it. Sit down to get the job done.

Sometimes we must use a public toilet or one in someone else's home. If it is a public toilet, wipe the seat off, and then cover the area with a sanitary paper (if provided) or strips of toilet paper before sitting on it. You never know if people before you had good or bad sanitary habits, and you don't know if someone had a skin disease. There is one place I recommend males raise the seat to urinate, and that is in filthy public toilets, if you find yourself having to use one.

Both sexes should wipe their urinary duct outlet afterward to prevent urine dribbles from getting on their underwear and pubic hair, just as they wipe their rectums to remove feces smear. Think about this: you are relaxing with someone who is fond of you. And after a while, they recline to rest their head on your lap. Suddenly, they sense the smell of an old stinky urinal, or feces. Talk about a turn off.

What would work faster? Keep yourself clean, and change your underwear often.

One common lazy and dirty habit is the way many people change a baby's dirty diaper. They wipe up the baby's bottom with a corner of the diaper that looks rather clean. Next, they put another diaper on the baby without washing the child and applying Vaseline or some other protective barrier oil on their child's bottom. Then they wonder why their child cries all the time. Lots of them act like they can't figure out how their child gets the big open sores on their bottom either. To protect their tender skin from the harsh acids of digestion, thorough cleansing and the application of an oil-base barrier cream is vitally important. This should always be done before applying a clean diaper.

I used to get after people for changing their babies' diapers in this slack and inconsiderate way. However, after the years I spent working as an ambulance attendant, I learned that plenty of adults need the same advice for themselves. During those years I, like all other self-respecting attendants, learned to fear people who were hygienically filthy in any way. I saw some startling bad hygienic characteristics from people of every walk of life.

Sometimes my fellow attendant and I were asked to assist the hospital staff to get the injured or sick patient ready for examination and treatment by a doctor because they were short-staffed. Plenty of times when assisting, I saw people dressed in clean, good-looking, and stylish clothing but wearing grotesque underwear. They had not been properly cleaning themselves, and some had sores like diaper rashes too.

What hope is there for adults to change a baby properly when they do not have the sense to care for their own groin and rectum areas? Considering these factors, it is little wonder why so many adults complain about hemorrhoid symptoms of inflamed rectum tissue. Also, it is easy to see how companies that sell products for these symptoms can be doing such a booming business.

Some people spend lots of time and money to look attractive. They buy new clothes all the time, but their underwear and bodies do not compliment their surface looks. This circumstance parallels a statement made by Jesus in Matthew 23:27. There it says, "Woe unto you scribes and Pharisees, hypocrites! For ye are like unto whited sepulchers which indeed appear beautiful outward, but are within full of dead men's bones, and of all uncleanness."

When you notice yourself starting to dig or scratch at your bottom, you should take it as an early warning alarm. This is a signal that you should immediately start paying more attention to cleaning and caring for yourselves after using the washroom. A description on how to clean ourselves after using a washroom should not have to be written here; everyone should have gotten this training from their parents long before they even started school. However, there are some adults who wipe across their anus, spreading the feces smear instead of cleaning it off themselves. They should be cleaning themselves by wiping toward their anus and away from the center of it in a motion away from their body.

There are some people who have a habit that is even worse yet. Instead of reaching down from one side or behind themselves, they reach down between their legs and wipe the feces smear from their bottom, across their perineum area, and even over their genital area. Also, in general, those who do a lousy job of cleaning themselves after using a toilet are also the people who usually use a lot more toilet paper. They are far more prone to plug the toilet. I sometimes wonder if they have a psychological fear that their hand might touch the feces. So to guard against that possibility, they use far more tissue paper than is required. I think they do it to insure a thick barrier is between their hand and their rectum, which is also a part of their skin organ. It is difficult to clean yourself properly with a fluffy pile of tissue paper like a pillow or glove.

When you go to the washroom, cleaning yourself is a vitally important job that needs to be done properly with concern to do it right every time. And that includes washing your hands every time you use the toilet. An absent-minded or lazy cleaning habit is a very serious threat to your health. Also, anyone associated with you intimately or otherwise is at risk too if you do not use proper hygiene. Filthy habits promote spreading of bacteria that cause painful infections in peoples' sex organs.

Another problem for women to consider is wiping yourself after urinating with soft tissue paper. If you engage in sexual intercourse afterward and some of the cellulose fibers of the paper comes apart and adheres to your labia, it may get propelled into your vagina by your partner's penis. This can cause an irritating discomfort for both parties, and foreign material on sensitive organ tissue can cause infection that can lead to chronic menstrual problems. This is a correctable problem that, along with other benign infections causing a mild illness with good prognosis for recovery, has instead caused many women to be sent for a hysterectomy.

We all know that tiny wood slivers really irritate our skin when they get imbedded in it. We also know that if they are not removed, they can cause the area to fester from infection. This festering is caused from the irritation of cellulose fiber in tissue, which is wood that paper is made of. If microscopic cellulose fibers get imbedded in sensitive moist body cell tissues, they can cause irritation that may require medical treatments, including surgeries.

Therefore, make sure you are clean before engaging in sexual intercourse. Rinse out a warm terry cloth to clean your genital area, and make sure your partner is clean too. This is a good habit to get into before and after sharing sexual intimacy. Another good reason is nobody likes sleeping on a wet bed. So be a gentleman for your partner's comfort. Get up and get her a warm damp cloth to freshen up with after sharing sexual pleasure.

People who neglect to properly clean their bodies and wash their hands after using a bathroom are a big health threat. It not only affects their health, but it also threatens the health of others. Problems like scratching your skin afterward, causing the bacteria under your fingernails to become imbedded in your skin. Others who neglect to wash their hands before preparing food or nibbling at it can cause harmful bacteria to spread in themselves and others.

Always wash your hands after going to the bathroom and before meals no matter where you are or what you are doing. And use forethought about wanting your body to be clean before and after making love. Get in the habit of keeping yourself clean.

Don't Neglect Your Oral Cavity

There is another hygiene concern that can be a potential danger to health and life if it is not properly maintained. That is your oral cavity. The human mouth can be a critical breeding area for bad bacteria if it is neglected. Most people brush their teeth on a regular basis; however, this alone is not good enough, especially if your teeth are too close together for a toothbrush to get to the gums between them. Trapped food between your teeth can harbor rotting food material that can incubate harmful bacteria. Flossing your teeth on a regular basis, especially after eating meat that requires vigorous chewing, is vital.

When I learned to floss my teeth, I experienced a shocking revelation. I had just finished brushing my teeth, and my mouth felt totally refreshed. Then I used a floss wand to start flossing my teeth. Suddenly I smelled the foul odor of decayed food. On the floss string, there was a small piece of meat that had been putting pressure between my molars for a couple of days. It was frightening for me to realize I had lived with such a septic system working between my teeth.

Since I started flossing my teeth many years ago, I seldom catch a cold. And if I do get a touch of a cold, it is gone in a couple of days. I have not required another filling or a tooth pulled since then.

There should be a lot of discipline exercised by everyone in keeping their oral cavity clean for lots of reasons. One concern is your tongue. The taste buds on your tongue should be brushed when you brush your teeth as another precaution to prevent catching a cold. And you should rinse your mouth out after brushing your teeth by swishing water around in your mouth so you can flush the areas between your gums and lips and to get all the toothpaste solution out of your mouth. This is important because toothpaste can give you a stomachache if it is swallowed.

I have learned from experience that gargling requires caution. Mouthwash solutions are made with the idea of killing bacteria. This can have good and bad effects on your health. There is a protective bacterium that lives in your throat to protect you against harmful bacteria, but if the friendly bacterium is killed off by germicidal mouthwash, you may become sick. I found myself getting a sore throat and a cold after each time I use germicidal mouthwashes as a quick fix against having bad breath. Now I only gargle with water or warm water with some salt if I have a sore throat.

Kissing can be a pleasant experience if those involved have clean mouths. Otherwise, any number of health-threatening complications can arise from the transfer of harmful bacteria. Therefore, keep your mouth as reasonably clean as you can; always brush and floss your teeth at least once daily, and replace your tired old toothbrush at least once every three months.

Cleanliness in Suboptimum Circumstances

If you have the misfortune to be living under filthy conditions beyond your control, then you have a problem that I experienced several times in my life. From my experiences, I can tell you that if your attitude is *I want to keep myself clean,* then you can, even if you are surrounded by filth.

At one point in my life, after running my own business for five years, I suddenly found myself bankrupt. I was ineligible for unemployment insurance benefits, and the only welfare benefit I could access was to live in a hostel. It seemed to me the other people living there had no spirit of dignity about themselves. There was only one toilet, one bathtub, and one sink to be used by about two dozen men. The place was very old with a musky odor that gave it a vulgar feeling. When people used the bathroom, they left it as they found it:

dirty. There was no incentive or personal self-will to even attempt to change the situation. It was an environment of broken spirits and depression.

All the men did was cuss and swear. They spoke sometimes jokingly and sometimes with serious intent about immoral, savage, and revengeful thoughts (molesting women, getting drugs and alcohol, and beating on someone) for momentary relief of their bitterness and frustration. Their self-respect, if they ever had any, was gone. I tried to encourage some of them but found they were lazy tramps who would never dream of investing a cent of their money to better themselves educationally or in any other way.

Most of these men had spent their lives looking for an easy spot to be sponsored by the government or whatever. Although some of them had been sponsored to go to school, they had to put out responsible effort to go with the course. Unwilling to take on responsibilities, like staying straight and studying, many of them had dropped out of upgrading or trade schools for the second or third time.

There's no such place as an easy spot in this world. The search for an easy spot is harder work than just doing hard work, which is always a rewarding adventure. It takes hard work and incentive on your part. And the place to start this is with a self-respecting attitude. You must adopt an attitude that you are going to be a decent person hygienically and morally. No matter what your circumstances are, decide to endeavor to do good. After over thirty years of living a life full of problems, I have concluded the following about personal morality:

A morally decent thinking and acting person will, by his or her mindfulness, remain as such under bad or indecent circumstances too. And an immoral person will show what they are by the way they persistently act.

Because of the environment that I was in, I decided only to eat and sleep at the hostel. Although it was the middle of winter, getting up early in the morning, I walked about six blocks to a clean bathroom at a hotel lobby. There, I cleaned myself up for the day's business of finding a job. However, my first job was to clean the bathroom to show an appreciative attitude so the owner will not get discouraged about keeping it clean for customers like me.

After you finish washing and brushing your teeth, etc., there is no need to leave a mess for the next person. Rinse the washcloth out and wipe up the sink then rinse the cloth out again. If there are splatters on the mirror, it is usually unnecessary to use a store-bought cleaner. One of the best glass cleaners you can get is in the washcloth you just rinsed out: water.

Water is a solvent and is not toxic to the environment. Wipe the mirror with the moist cloth, and dry it right away with a dry towel. You may be surprised to see how clean and crystal clear the mirror will look. After I discovered that, I never bought window cleaners again.

If you are a decent person, then you are going to be decent and respectful toward everybody else no matter what your personal circumstances are.

Hygiene from the Inside Out

Most undesirable body odors can be kept under control with sensible dietary habits for good health. If you over-indulge eating unhealthy substances, you are feeding yourself pure garbage. And that is the impression you will express to hygienically conscientious people. A good example is smoking. What is going on at the cell level of your body when you smoke? One way to get an amplified preview of how bad it can get is to go visit a cancer ward. Go into the room of a patient reeking of rotting flesh with gaping cancer sores.

There is nothing sexually attractive about consuming garbage and smelling like it, and there is nothing sexually attractive about being too physically unfit to perform well sexually because of smoking or other drugs.

If you smoke and seriously want to quit, I strongly suggest you read the book *Easy Way to Stop Smoking* by Allen Carr. I never smoked but I have seen other people stop smoking without any anxiety after reading the book. Curious, I decided to read the book and was impressed. It is an amazing book that should easily work for anyone really interested in butting out.

Some people bathe in poison and do not even know it. To put on a hint of perfume is okay. However, it is quite something else when a person uses so much that it is literally an irritating and offensive stench to other people and poisonous to your own health. (A perfume factory is one of the worst-smelling places on earth.) If you want to use perfume, learn how to use it properly in moderation. Then you will be as pleasant to be around as fresh flowers. Still, simply keeping yourself clean is far better for your health.

People who use liniments and ointments for aches and pains and then try to smother the smell of the medication with perfume need to know they are probably just making the problem worse.

Skin covered with makeup suffocates from not being able to breathe. Consider what you are doing when you think of using it. It may make you look dazzling for a few years, but it does not take long before you end up with premature wrinkles. Those wrinkles inspire you to use more makeup more often to cover them up. You end up painting a new face on the good one you ruined, trying to look super beautiful. Be natural; don't try to be something you are not. "War paint" wages war with your face.

Another factor to consider before using perfumes, ointments, and mascara is: What chemicals are in the products that you are considering using? Find out if your body has any allergic reaction to it before using it. Otherwise, you might be gradually making yourself sick with skin problems or other symptoms, and you may never find out what is causing or has caused it.

Hygiene in Your Environment

Are your home and car clean enough that inviting people in won't lead to embarrassment? Every aspect about you expresses what type of person you are.

When I was single, I made it a rule to always leave my apartment clean. I was always able to enjoy relaxing in it when I returned and would never feel embarrassed about inviting anyone over at any time. If, for some reason, you can't leave your home clean, at least clean up the bathroom and the kitchen before you go out. They indicate, more than anything else, what type of person you are.

And who does not enjoy cruising in a clean machine? New or old, keep your vehicle attractively cleaned, especially inside. Even if you cannot afford to fix up the outside, keep the inside clean. This will express your concern about what is close to your body, and it is not expensive. I've got into some vehicles that smelled awful from people using the floor for a long-term garbage can. What may have been crawling around living in there, I hate to think. But if that is the way someone keeps their vehicle, how do they keep themselves?

If you clean your home or your body in a lazy and incomplete way, then it is still not clean after you finish working at cleaning it. People who don't clean in the corners (or behind furniture and appliances) on a regular basis are not thorough cleaners and often have the same attitude about cleaning themselves. Middle-of-the-floor cleaners are shunned by hygienically conscious people.

Some people use the same old filthy scrub water until they are finished washing the floor or dishes. These people are homogenizing the dirt instead of removing it. When my mother left her home as a teenager, she went to the city to find work. She stayed with a woman who ran a rooming house for porters who worked on the railroad. One day, she scrubbed a floor for the landlady before they had supper. During dinner, the woman held up the scrub cloth that my mother had been using and said, "When the scrub cloth is as clean as this after you have finished using it, then you know the floor is thoroughly clean too." The reason the scrub cloth was so clean was because my mother had changed her scrub water as often as was required to keep it reasonably clean and rinsed the floor after scrubbing it.

My mother taught us to always have a high respect for our property and to have that same respect for everyone else's property. When I graduated from high school, I asked the people at a car rental if I could rent a car from them. The agent said, "We do not rent cars to anyone under the age of twenty-five."

I hounded him about needing a car for my grad so much that he went against his company policy and rented me a new red Dodge Charger with my mother's co-signature. I was so excited that I couldn't have felt better if I had won a million dollars. Anyway, I went to my grad and after grad party and had a great time, but I kept in mind my mother's teaching to have full respect for other people's things and kept it clean.

The next day, I took it to the car wash to have it thoroughly cleaned inside and out, along with a hot wax treatment and fueled it up before I returned it. When I arrived, the agent rushed out to examine the car. He had been worried sick because he had stuck his neck out by going against company policy. He was surprised and pleased that the car had been well looked after and was already filled with gas. The manager was there too, and he gave me a special card that allowed me to rent a car from them any time. I had experienced my first big benefit from having respect for other people and their property.

I don't know what inspired him to rent the car to me in the first place. However, I suspect it had a lot to do with my mannerisms—from the way I spoke and dressed to the way I carried myself. My mother taught us to never look down on others, but also to never feel inferior about ourselves, either. When a person carries themselves in a downtrodden manner, people sense it, and this has a negative influence on how they will interact with you.

Every aspect, positive or negative, about our spiritual hygiene and attitude has profound effects on what we will or will not get out of life. When I meditate on my first experience of renting a car and several other highlights of that nature in my life, I always come to the same conclusion: that my expressed attitude of respect had more to do with why I got whatever I did than anything else.

Junk

Junk puts a stranglehold on our free spirit, causing a form of depression that cripples our ability to function. It can get so bad we feel like we exist for nothing because from day to day, we can't accomplish anything. We have to clean up just to get something done, but if we only move the junk from one place to another, we soon find ourselves having to move it again. The more clutter we have, the less enthusiasm we have for dealing with it and the less enthusiasm we have for getting anything else done while all that clutter is in the way.

The weight of all this junk can propel us into a serious downward spiral. Worse, we become servants to our junk, and it becomes lord of the manor. There's an option though: we can get rid of all that clutter and reap the benefits, whether those benefits are financial (sell our excess to those who can use it), philanthropic (donate it to a worthy cause or give it to someone who needs it), or therapeutic (the simple joy of an uncluttered space). Once we realize junk is our enemy, we can evict it and reclaim our home. Consider this scenario. Junk is piled everywhere including on chairs. You want to sit down, but first, you have to find another place for the junk that's residing there before you can have a place to sit. The junk has the authority, not you. You have to serve the junk with a new place to stay first before you can occupy that chair. So who is the servant? This example has led me to believe junk is nothing less than demonic spirits antagonizing you, so evict it permanently and end the anxiety. Investing junk in the dump bank gives you high interest in peace of mind.

During a visit to a coworker's home, I noticed everything was neatly in its designated place. When I commented to him about how organized his place was, he replied that whenever anything in his home hadn't served a useful purpose within thirty days, he gave it away or threw it out. He did not tolerate being a slave to junk; everything either served him or it was turfed. He was certainly the king of his home, not a servant to the junk lord.

Too much of anything is a misery to deal with.

Mind Junk

While we are on the subject of junk, consider this: to let go of bad things that have happened to us is like throwing away useless junk. When we hold fast to past pain, constantly dwelling on it, we allow it to rule us. I know that sometimes it is very hard to let it go, but we must if we ever hope to restore peace to our souls. Think about this. Holding resentment is like taking poison and expecting someone else to be harmed by it. The only one suffering is you, the victim, not the victimizer.

Naturally Clean

When people want to get across the idea of something being clean and fresh, they use pictures of nature in virgin landscape scenes undisturbed by man's pollution. Everything emphasizes the environment as being alive and clean and innocent.

Picture a fertile world with crystal clear water flowing over rocks and lush green foliage accented with innocent herbivorous creatures such as fawns and butterflies. You feel like you would love to enter this scene and stay there forever, enjoying the cleanliness, peace, and tranquility. The fertility of this marvelous work comes from Almighty God, our Father in heaven's paradise garden.

In the garden of your body and your home, wouldn't you like to keep them hygienically clean to the best of your ability as undisturbed nature does? Wouldn't you rather enjoy this environment than live in a toxic brew of unhealthy chemicals? If so, send an email to healthiswealth888@yahoo.com, telling them you would like to learn how this is possible. They'd be happy to share with you what they've learned about this.

Cleanliness offers many healthy rewards, including the respect of others. And you may benefit from the most positively enjoyable sexual experience possible when you do meet the love of your life, especially if they practice good toiletry and hygiene mentally and physically in every way they can too.

Moral Values and Respect

The moral values that you believe in and live by determine what you are worth to any relationship—business, family, friends, or sexual partner. We need to examine the way we live and act on an ongoing basis because we are presented with demoralizing temptations every day of our lives.

To prevent ourselves from sliding toward barbarism, we need to take time out for self-examination; find someplace quiet, without any electronic entertainment or other distraction, examine the way we have been acting and set goals to improve our attitudes and principles.

Some of the questions we should ask ourselves:

- How do I treat other people?
- Would I like other people to treat me the way I treat any other person?
- Do I demand more of others than I demand of myself? (This is extremely important to

the health of your marriage. However, practicing fairness in your marriage will not work in a marriage if you do not also practice it in every other aspect of your life.)

- Do I express prejudice or hatred toward any group of people, nationality, family, or individual such as my boss or spouse?

- Do I have any kind of hatred or resentment for men, women, or children? (Don't laugh at these questions as being nonsense. They are often the subtle beginnings of what causes immeasurable misery to not only everyone around us but to ourselves also. We can and do become victims poisoned by our own evil hatred toward others, so it is important to think about it.)

- Do I use, abuse, criticize, or treat anyone as though they are less than me in any way?

- Am I a yes-man, laughing along with any belittling gossip joke made about others? (It is vital to have a mind of your own and stand tall to support decent moral respect for all others.)

- What respect do I have for other people's feelings, beliefs, and ideas?

- What do I know about those I am biased about? (Often, we don't know much about anyone we have biased feelings about, and what we think we know about them is probably warped. It's important to ponder these points before we judge others.)
- In all honesty, would I be any different than those I am biased about if I had experienced the same past life and culture that they have lived—such as being raised by parents with a prejudiced and hateful nature toward any person or group of people?
- Has someone trampled on my feelings, causing me to be bitter?
- Am I taking revenge on others who are innocent of crimes I've been a victim of?
- What am I if I victimize innocent people because I have been victimized? (Is this justified? Is it right? What profit is there to us if we hurt others as we have been hurt?)

The above questions are similar to some extent. However, what we want to do is *look at our moral values from every possible angle.*

Examine yourself honestly. Are you lacking respect for other people in any way? Following are some true stories that may help you take a deeper and more critical look at yourself as a person.

Imagine yourself as a teenager, being asked by your friends if you would like to go to a drive-in movie in your car (because they do not have one). When you pick them up, you are surprised to find out they're bringing their dates.

At the movie, your guests are heavily into sexual foreplay and ask you if you would mind going for some refreshments for everybody. They offer to pay for it, but you know they are getting you out of the way to use your car privately and using you as their go-fetch-it flunkey too.

This is the most bitter experience for the one left out, isn't it? Have the dignity to respect other people's feelings. Not only in a situation as described above but in all circumstances. When you're with others, do not carry on a conversation with only one of them. Every one of us is very sensitive to being left out, whether we admit to this or not. If you are out with your lover and a friend, then go as just friends. Do not exclude the odd one out, and do not show off your sexual enjoyment in front of them. It could lead to your death as it almost did after the movie scene in the story above.

The teenager who was driving the car felt so ticked off by the whole affair that he left the drive-in driving like a madman. Yes, I felt like committing suicide, and the others in the car had no choice but to go for the ride to their death with me. Luckily, there was no accident in my case. However, how often might that be the unknown reason for, especially young people, ending up in high-speed disastrous crashes that land them in the morgue? As a couple, do not show off your sexual enjoyment in front of other people who are alone.

Have you ever been a role model of any one of these characters mentioned above in a former situation in your life?

As a nonwhite person, I have experienced the prejudice of others. However, no matter who we are or what we think we are, most of us have some problems with being prejudiced. I know I have had biased feelings about other people myself, and that it takes a lot of work to overcome deep-rooted prejudices that are always the results of only one thing: ignorance.

The only way we can do something to improve the problem is by educating ourselves. We need to recognize why we and other people are crippled with prejudices. This usually dissolves the prejudices we have. Often learning about people leads to admiration and respect for customs we formerly disliked. As I said before, we all need to do an honest evaluation of ourselves from time to time, without distractions, to make sure we are not becoming disrespectful of others.

Devaluing Others' Pain for Entertainment

In the spring of 1980, I was in a class renewing my industrial first aid certificate. While we practiced our bandaging on one another, the two nurses in the class got into a conversation about the latest movie fad: watching people being tortured to death in pornographic snuff movies. These nurses said the movies looked very realistic, and, to my disgust, they acted as though they found them entertaining.

People were getting these movies from black market dealers. I never saw any of those movies, but people who were talking about them back then said they wondered if the actors were actually victims being tortured to death for real in those snuff movies. Some believed it was the only way that such realistic effects could have been filmed. And incredibly, the nurses casually mentioned that fact as well. Would the black market spend millions of dollars to make realistic scenes of gruesome torturers, or would they kidnap innocent victims to slaughter, minimizing the cost?

I don't know if the nurses were trying to impress the young men they were talking to or what. However, I know I would not want a person who could enjoy that sort of thing for a girlfriend. And it would scare the hell out of me to learn that a nurse with that type of moral attitude and disrespect for people was looking after me while I was helplessly sick.

Who knows what happens to our children who go missing or are abandoned to strangers? What happens to children or teenagers who leave home because there is no love for them there?

Some children are victims of parents or guardians who sexually molest them. What can happen to them when they run away with no place to go only to be snared by others who are indifferent to human suffering?

- What moral qualities do you have, and what are you promoting if you spend your money to get pornographic and snuff movies?
- If you buy them, are you any better than the evildoers that make them?

- Do you try to look popular in front of your friends by carrying on conversations about any kind of violent movies or entertainment?

It does not take any brains or guts to practice degenerate immoral ways. However, it takes respectable moral perseverance in a person to live a decent and clean life. As such, you must be forever concerned about what you invest your money in for entertainment and what you encourage others to support.

Are you promoting a way of thinking that could or will cause misery or death to other people? Do you enjoy watching detective shows displaying gruesome events or so-called organized fighting sports, where people are being beaten, etc.? What type of people laugh at the portrayal of inflicted pain and suffering? What type of heathens back in the days of the Roman Empire went to the stadiums, eager to watch defenseless innocent people being ripped apart and killed by lions and other wild creatures? If you were alive then, would you have gone there for what was then an accepted form of entertainment?

Gossip

No one should ever gossip about someone else's embarrassing moments, but we should rather be a Good Samaritan who privately helps protect the embarrassed person to the best of our ability. For example, if someone gets sick from food that didn't agree with them and unexpectedly soils their clothing from incontinence of some kind. Victims of these embarrassing moments in public sometimes can use help from a compassionate individual who silently helps and afterward never breathes a word of gossip to anyone else about what happened. Only degenerate mentalities gossip about others' embarrassing misfortunes.

Be respectful of others' privacy and need to secrecy about their embarrassing moments. Remember none of us can say assuredly that we will never find ourselves in a similar embarrassing state someday. Be kind and respectful of all others' need for dignity because nothing unfortunate about us should be exploited for public entertainment.

The Company We Keep

If you have a friend or spouse or someone you are engaged to whose aphrodisiac is violent entertainment, what lies in the future of your relationship? What kind of sincere trust is there with such a companion? How long would it be before an associate of yours with a mind like this starts exercising abusive behavior toward you or one of your loved ones? Maybe they will start abusing or molesting your children or spouse behind your back. Worse, it could be your spouse molesting your children and threatening them if they tell.

It is important to examine with critical attention the behavioral characteristics of those with whom we get involved. And if we have not ensured our own moral values are those of a sympathetic and caring person toward *all* other people, it is easier to become the victim of a coldhearted person. Blindly falling in love with someone can often be a tragic mistake. Therefore, you need to examine whether or not you take pleasure in violent entertainment.

Is something like a desire for revenge or wanting to be loved, causing you to find violent entertainment a stimulating replacement for what you lack? Do you think that saturating your mind with bitter, violent thoughts will improve your chances of meeting someone who will someday provide you with the sincere love you crave? Honestly evaluate your attitude. Remember that a successful marriage or friendship depends on two things: *finding* the right person and *being* the right person.

It is difficult to understand some people's moral values. People in general seem to be callous rather than sympathetic about the suffering they see others are experiencing, even sufferings that they themselves have experienced.

While the United States of America was at war with Vietnam, there were massive demonstrations everywhere against it. When I think of that war, I recall a famous photograph taken in 1972, which showed a South Vietnamese girl who had been badly burned in a napalm attack, running naked toward the photographer. She and the people she was travelling with had been mistaken by the South Vietnamese for the North Vietnamese enemy troops, from whom they were fleeing. This haunting image and the dreadful details behind it were a stark reminder of the innocent victims of war; people everywhere were horrified.

However, only a couple of years previous, I had seen people cheer at a similarly horrifying incident. The movie *Little Big Man* (starring Dustin Hoffman as

Jack Crabb) had just been released, dramatizing the same bitter realities of war. At one point in the show, General Custer and his soldiers were slaughtering the Cheyenne. Crabb's young wife was running from one of Custer's men, who was in hot pursuit on horseback. She was running huddled over her baby, trying to protect him from the hailstorm of bullets flying everywhere. The man on the horse intentionally planted a bullet square in the middle of her back.

I was stricken with grief thinking about it, imagining myself as one of the people being massacred or a father witnessing this happening to his little family, but what hurt worse than the show itself was the audience's reaction; a man's voice rang through the theatre: "Kill 'em all."

On the screen, the men on horseback pumped bullets into women and children as they fled in panic. *Boom! Boom! Boom!* And at the same time, it sounded like most of the people in the theatre cheered. My god, did I ever feel sick and shocked. I could not believe I heard what I heard. I was so stunned I sat dumbfounded with fear as to how mercilessly cold people can be toward one another. Especially since these same people were demonstrating strong opinions against the Vietnam War! I thank God I have never experienced anything like that again. However, it still haunts me that it even happened once.

It is little wonder there are so many divorces in this callous world when people have such little reverence for defenseless children and anyone else whose physical might is less than their own. The people in the theatre that day were a cold reminder of the heathens in the Roman Empire arenas. What honor is there between a husband and wife if their mental attitude is as those people's minds at that show? The movie had gone into much detail to express the placid, kind, and loving attitude of these people before showing General Custer's men slaughtering them so ruthlessly.

I often wonder if the people who were laughing at the brutality on the screen were intoxicated from years of watching violent movies. Many people entertain themselves with this sort of thing and then joke about it in casual conversation. Make it your sole entertainment and after a while, your heart becomes stone cold. How much violent entertainment can any decent person enjoy and still retain their good moral values?

Some people reading this might say, "Those were some sick people back then." I ask: Has anything changed for the better or is it worse? Today, people immerse themselves in virtual reality video games where zero mercy is to be shown for the hundreds or even thousands of people they kill in the games. Some of these games show the people in front of your gun crying out for mercy, but unless you desensitize yourself to their cries and kill them all, you lose the game.

Do not write a movie off as being *just* a movie, so there's no need to feel concern for suffering you see portrayed there. The violent games are not *just* violent games. Do you consider the news as *just* the news?

In 2011, I was at work with colleagues watching breaking news coverage of the tsunami that hit Japan. Newsfeed from a helicopter showed a car racing desperately to outrun the advancing tidal wave. One of my colleges burst out laughing. We were watching live coverage of hundreds of people losing their lives, but once again, I was hearing people laughing at other people's horrifying demise.

During the summer of 1971, I got a job moving office equipment and doing some work on a wharf and hired two students to help me. One was impatient to turn sixteen, return to the United States, and enlist to go to Vietnam. When I asked why, he said a lot of his older friends who had been there were now respected as war heroes because of their injuries like missing arms and legs. When the other student and I tried to reason with him, he provided a sick, degenerate reason that stunned me with dismay: he said he wanted to experience raping women and children like some of the men he knew bragged about. And from the way he talked, he clearly thought that I, being male, should understand that this was a reasonable normal way for men to want to treat the victims they've overpowered in a war.

After trying unsuccessfully to reason with him, I asked if he ever considered the risk he was taking of contracting sexual disease. He replied that although lots of soldiers got diseased from raping women, it didn't concern him. He told us that because the risk of being raped by American soldiers was so high, women in Vietnam were making cylindrical devices with razor blades like spokes inside them and placing these devices inside themselves so that their assailant's penises would be sliced upon penetration. This, too, was a risk he said he was willing to take, adding that soldiers were examining their victims for that risk now anyway before raping them.

That teenager was clearly a very sick individual. He was able to talk about his intentions with absolutely no concern for those he wanted to victimize. The more I tried to reason with him, the more distraught I became from listening to his replies. It left me bewildered, wondering how many men with that type of thinking enlist to go to wars anywhere in search of the opportunity to rape defenseless women and children.

If a man goes to war and molests women and children, like this fifteen-year-old was looking forward to doing, what will his mental state be when he returns home after the war is over? The first four books of the Holy Bible are about moral values and hygiene. During that time, God's people were at war against heathen nations. God warned his people not to do anything morally indecent while they were at war because when they returned to their homes, they would take the curses of such things back home with them. This warning makes perfectly good sense. How can a person nourish an appetite for violent rape without becoming permanently affected by it? Therefore, how intense is the curse against all nations that have allowed immoral behavior to be exercised by their soldiers in wars down through time?

I find people who are so immune to human suffering frightening to be associated with. This is especially so in a marriage. When a soldier returns home, their behavior is restricted, but their appetites haven't changed. This may be why they turn toward sexual molestation of those within their own family; these are the people they can control in secret. Once started, how far down through the generations of a family can this type of cursed behavior continue?

Two of my friends are women who grew up in foster care, one in British Columbia and the other on a farm in Alberta. Both became victims of sexual molestation at the hands of their foster fathers, and both foster fathers had their own teenage sons participate in gang rapes with them for years. Where did the fathers' attitudes come from? And what were these fathers teaching their sons to be?

The girls grew up like victims of war with no rights and no hope. They could not cry out for help because of the threats by their victimizers. In the early 1970s, complaints to government officials about this sort of abuse fell on deaf ears; these women's social workers didn't believe them and told them to keep their mouths shut.

Females are not the only victim of sexual molestation; many boys in sports and other activities have been victims of perverted adults in positions of responsibility. And problems like these are impossible to solve while some religious and political leaders of the world are themselves involved with this kind of wrongdoing. I cannot stress this strongly enough: *the moral values you believe in and live by determine what you are worth to any relationship, be it business, family, friend, or sexual partner.* We must continually examine our own behavior and make sure we safeguard our own morals.

One day, when I was a student, my girlfriend asked if we could go see a horror movie. We went and at one point, someone was brutally murdered by a horrible, frightening axe-wielding monstrosity. It was as vicious and horrifying as it gets, and I shuddered as I imagined such a fate. I had my arm around my girl-friend, and she turned to me calmly and said, "That bothers you, eh? It's just a movie."

Some people watch horror movies until they have no sensitivity left. Consider the cartoon *Tom and Jerry*, where one of them does something cruel to the other and laughs hysterically. Then in the next scene, they both are in friendly partnership against a rival. After successfully getting rid of the rival, they are back at doing vicious things to each other. I really question what's behind the brainwashing insanity presented to the general public by trying to normalize violence toward others.

It seems every day, there's another terrible story in the news of someone who went berserk and killed his or her family. You say it can't happen to you, that you have too much self-control to flip out like that.

Gradualism can transform any man, woman, or child into a savage beast. The only hope is, you must examine yourself now while you still can. But *will you?*

Do it while you are still in control of your own destiny. Meditate on your ways, and ask yourself again, "Does it bother me when I see violence done against others?"

Why not take time out right now to sit down and really think about it? Please stop and think about it now. Right now.

Did you just keep reading? Or did you stop to think about what you need to do to improve your attitude about things?

No time for peace right now? No hope? Remember: the moral values that you believe in and live by determine what you are worth to any relationship.

The Origin of Good and Evil

To understand the significance of this chapter, it is essential that you have first read the preceding chapters in the order presented. This chapter addresses a spiritual mentality that influences the promotion of hatred in our society. Its influence changes continually, always giving the impression of inspiring revelations. Although it doesn't harmonize with the laws of nature, there is a subtle attraction to this way of thinking that can blindside anyone who doesn't consciously guard themselves against following its destructive force.

The laws of nature function to produce a stress level of zero. Scientific research on this subject continues to find overwhelming evidence that these laws are logical, and that they are good for all of nature. Because we can regard them as the laws of a sane nature, we can also consider anything contrary to them as insane or illogical—leading not to the truth but rather to destructive deception. This insight will help you recog-

nize the difference between the natural good laws of nature and the source of corruption.

As far back as I can remember, I have meditated on the cause of (or reasoning behind) the acts of cruelty I'd seen inflicted by one person on another. The perpetrators were usually watching to see that they did not get caught at what they were doing, which tells me they knew full well that what they were doing was wrong but fully intended to do it anyway. They knew better but chose to be defiant against what they understood to be right. In other words, their acts were insane. They deliberately chose to defiantly reject righteousness to embrace unrighteousness. That's insanity.

Another sad thing I have noticed is that the clear majority of people prefer to hide in a crowd that is following a leader. Many of them would never do alone what they are willing to do with the gang. They are mindlessly following whatever leader they have chosen to follow. Why does this happen? What force is at work causing people to keep doing things that go against what they know is right and good? Where did all the evil insanity embraced by so many people come from?

To get an understanding of why all the wickedness exists, we need to examine its history, just as scientists explore the origin and behavior of a subject to understand what it is, why it is, and what it does.

The Holy Bible has been proven to be a resource of dependable historical information. Therefore, it would be biased to withhold documentation about the origin of evil that is described in its pages. Here, I have paraphrased some of what it says about the history of good and evil: *First was the good that was Almighty God Jehovah or Yahweh, who never began but always was the living God. And the Word of God, Jesus Christ, who is the personification of God's love. And the Holy Ghost that is the entity of God's spirit influence on us if we will choose to invite it in us.*

Confusing? The best way I know how to describe this is by the equation *1 x 1 x 1 = 1.*

An atom consists of three entities. They are electrons, protons, and neutrons; all are required for an atom to exist. We have a spirit (life force), a soul (personality), and we live in a body. These three together make up the oneness of each of us. Together, the three dimensions of God made everything that was created in the heavens and on the earth. This is stated in the New Testament (John 1:1–3), and many other passages in the Bible clarify this fact.

Angels created by God are spirit beings of God. The angel sons of God, like Himself, will never perish and live forever. All God's angels were supposed to worship Him (have respect for Him and His law). And part of that law was that they were not made with a natural purpose to engage in sexual intercourse for fertility because they are complete within themselves.

He created one angel, Lucifer, full of wisdom and perfect in beauty. Lucifer was the most highly blessed angel son, blessed with more perfections than any other angel. While Jehovah God created Adam and Eve to be the caretakers of the garden of Eden. This garden was to be developed by man until it covered the whole earth. Originally, Lucifer was to be the overseer of the garden. But Lucifer, already the most highly blessed of the angels, craved even more; he became disrespectful and greedy. He wanted his Father's place as ruler over the universe.

Puffed up about himself, he decided that because of his brightness and cherished appearance, he should be worshipped above all else. Lucifer wanted to be worshipped by the universe rather than see his Father, Jehovah God, the creator of the universe, being honored with this respected position.

And because he wanted man and God's spirit angel sons to respect him over his Father, he challenged God that man would prefer to worship him above God. To test man's respect, God placed a tree in the midst of the garden that Adam and Eve were not to touch. This was the test to show whether man would have respect for the Creator, Jehovah God Almighty, or the creation, Lucifer.

The garden was supposed to be a place for all men to live forever in perfect health and happiness in a paradise garden on earth. Lucifer wanted to turn man against Jehovah God, so he appeared as a snake before Eve and told her God was withholding wisdom from her and Adam by forbidding them to eat the fruit of that one tree. He said that God knew if they ate the fruit, their eyes would be opened to knowledge of good and evil, and they would become gods themselves. He said God was hiding freedom and knowledge from them, freedom and knowledge that they had a right to enjoy. And he also assured Eve that if she ate of the forbidden fruit, it would not cause her destruction in death as God had warned them it would.

The Bible shows in many places that Almighty God is not a suppressor of freedom. From the beginning, Jehovah God gave all mankind and all His spirit angels of the heavens, the freedom to do the will of their own minds and hearts. They had the freedom to be good by honoring God's righteousness, which resulted in personal reward through giving and receiving love in its purest form. However, if any one of them were to freely choose to be a resister against Jehovah God's righteousness, then their desire not to honor their Father's living Word would end in their own destruction.

Instead of standing fast to the truth, Lucifer challenged the righteousness and rightfulness of Jehovah God's sovereignty over the universe. And so he was given the name Satan, and he also became known as the devil. Satan is the spirit creator of deceit, fear and lies, plus he is the foremost slanderer of God. In short, Lucifer created evil and hatred and became the insane one, Satan. He became the god of evil by creating evil.

Satan hates anything living that respects Almighty God, especially man because man could enjoy intimate sexual love of which Satan was not meant to partake. And with God as the referee over Satan's challenge that man would rather worship him than God Almighty. God allowed the earth to become flooded because of what Satan's demonic angels were doing in Noah's time. They were coming down to earth to have sex and children with man's daughters, so God allowed the earth that became filled with exceeding evil to flood to wipe them out. You can read about this in chapters six and seven of Genesis in the Holy Bible.

God did not make zombies or living clones with no free will of their own. Almighty God, being true to His word, has never been a suppressor of any spirit or soul to exercise their personal free will. As such, God Almighty gave Satan a chance to prove his theory that God's spirit angels and mankind would prefer to worship him, a creation, rather than their Father, the Creator Himself. Two more crystal clear examples of Satan's full intentions are the story of Satan putting Job to the test and when he tried to convince Jesus to bow down and worship him.

Eve was tricked into believing that God was being deceitful to them and ate fruit from the tree. The effect of eating of that forbidden fruit caused Eve to entice her husband, Adam, to eat the fruit too. And he did, even though he knew full well that it was wrong. They had freely chosen to place their confidence in Satan's lies rather than in their Creator's righteousness. They had disrespected their Creator's sovereignty over them.

Therefore, God removed them from the paradise garden he had made for them and let mankind follow the way of their hearts in a world where they would not be able to live forever. Mankind had chosen to live by their personal choice to experience, knowing good and evil. Since they had failed the test of obedience to the Father Creator, Satan was given the right to rule over the earth and mankind for a time. This was to provide an opportunity for all mankind to experience the values of good and evil: respect for Almighty God's righteousness or for Satan's insanity.

Satan did manage to trick the first people on earth to go against the laws of God. That caused them to suffer and die. As they became imperfect, it caused them and all their decedents to suffer the consequences of their decision. We are suffering too from the wrongs of our ancestors, all the way back to Adam and Eve who were made perfect. They were supposed to have everlasting life in perfection, but they became imperfect when they went against God's advice that was for their own safety to experience Satan's influence over them.

Adam and Eve made the same choice many people choose today. They go against what they know to be good advice to experience bad things. Their conscience of righteousness tells them *not* to go with that which is bad. However, all too often, people rebel against righteousness. They choose to experience the spirit of evil abilities in themselves rather than the spirit of good in them.

Unfortunately, many choose to indulge in deadly mind-enslaving drugs, health-threatening casual sex, and anything else against the Ten Commandments that they consider exciting and trendy. However, these traits aren't natural. The more anyone engages in unrighteous acts, the weaker their resistance becomes against unrighteousness and the easier it becomes to ignore your good conscience.

The statement "there is no honor among thieves" holds true for Satan because there is zero love in him. He hates everyone, including his loyal evildoers. On the other hand, loving, benevolent people are your friends even if they don't know you. So what kind of fool are you if you do evil against your friends to cater to Satan?

In Good Conscience

The good conscience is a part of our natural instinct to protect our own welfare, the welfare of others, and everything else in nature. The more one follows the advice of the good conscience, the stronger it becomes; and the weaker the evil consciousness becomes, as does its ability to control us. Conversely, anyone who chooses to devote their thoughts to the evil conscience in them makes it grow stronger, and eventually they lose their ability to sense their good conscience's advice. Basically, whichever conscience you decide to dwell on or nourish will grow strong in you, and the other one will wither.

I like the way my friend Frank George describes the spirit of our morals as two little voices. The good little voice sits on one shoulder, giving you good advice to consider; the bad little voice sits on your other shoulder, trying to entice you to enjoy an experience that is not in your best interest. An important difference between these two voices is that the good little voice quietly offers advice without being pushy (like the gentleman God is by allowing us to freely choose for ourselves from the good advice that is politely offered); the bad little voice tries aggressively to entice you, using the same pushy "lying salesman" attitude Satan used when he was tricking Eve.

When people have gone wrong far enough; giving them good advice is like talking to a brick wall. That bad little voice becomes an overpowering monster. Dwelling on evil thoughts and entertainment long enough leaves them unable to see any value in doing anything righteous.

People who listen more to the good conscience tend to live longer lives because of the happiness in them, while those who choose to pursue unrighteousness become filled with stressful poisons that destroy the quality of their life.

The righteous conscience of love was created by Jehovah God; the evil conscience hate was created by Satan, the devil.

To Everything, a Season

The Holy Bible tells us the time God allotted for Satan to prove man would rather worship him is almost over. Most of the signs of the end of his time, described in the book of Revelations, have already happened.

Satan's rule was not denied by Jesus Christ. This is emphasized in Luke 4:5–7, where Satan tries to tempt Jesus Christ. Satan offers Jesus all the earth, that He has the right to rule over at present if Jesus will just get down and worship him. Jesus didn't deny that Satan had the authority to do that at that time; however, Jesus refused to be tempted. He showed His intent to remain patient until the time when Satan's allotted time is up, which is now almost upon us.

Jehovah God will end Satan's corrupt rulership, granting reign instead to Jesus Christ's righteous governance. Under Christ's rule, the earth will be restored back to a paradise garden that the Bible says will be even better than the original garden of Eden and will be eternal. It will never end, and death will be no more.

Jesus Christ our Savior is the only begotten Son of Jehovah God Almighty because even though He was with His Father, God Almighty, from the beginning, He was later born of an earthly virgin mother, Mary. Since the earth was cursed, Jesus had to come from God—not man—as the fathering parent to pass the test against Satan in a body of flesh and blood. Jesus was born to experience what it would be like to be tempted by Satan in a body of flesh and blood, as Adam and Eve were, without failing the test to remain righteous. He succeeded, remaining sinless for the whole time of His life on earth. Therefore, the death He suffered from Satan's advocates was unjust, so God Almighty resurrected Jesus Christ from the dead.

By going against God, Adam caused all men to suffer with death that we inherited from him. Jehovah God wanted to give Adam's decedents the same hope that Adam had. Therefore, Jehovah God's Son, Jesus Christ, volunteered to come to earth, be born of flesh and blood, live a perfect life, and die as a perfect ransom sacrifice for our sins because of His unjust death. He lived the only perfect life ever lived by a man. And that gave Him authority to redeem us from our sins. They, God and Jesus Christ, want to give us the same opportunity as Adam and Eve had before they sinned. That is why the resurrection promise is written in the Holy Bible.

Only Jesus Christ could pass this test because we, who have been born of Adam, are not perfect. However, Jesus's Father, God, who is perfect, made it possible for Jesus to be the same as His Father, which He proved to be.

When Jesus was crucified, He had suffered an unjust death instigated by Satan. Due to what Satan did to Jesus Christ, who had lived a perfect life, Jesus received the right that Adam from the garden of Eden lost. That right made Jesus Christ the Second Adam. He received the power from His Father, Jehovah God, to resurrect man from death when He takes over as ruler over man. This is why Jesus Christ is known as the sacrificial Lamb; He bought us out of bondage of death with His blood. Jesus Christ gave us back the same hope for our resurrected life to come, as Adam and Eve had of eternal life, living in a paradise environment.

It is because of what Jesus Christ did for us that we will be raised from death to a second chance for everlasting life. A life where, if we are thankful for the loving gift God Almighty has provided for us through the shedding of His only begotten Son's blood, we can expect to enjoy. A life the Holy Bible promises will be so awesome that we do not have the mind today to imagine how good it will be.

Now that you have read this paraphrased account of the Biblical story on the origin of evil, can you see why all that you can see is the way it is in this world? Lies to cause confusion are Satan's weapon. Destruction of Almighty God's creation is Satan's goal, and it's all because of his unjust envy to his Creator.

See to it that you are not supporting Satan's motive. It's up to all of us to judge ourselves and correct our attitudes rather than suffer the consequences.

Don't Let Insanity Rule You

The living God Almighty is the creator of us. Therefore, His law is supreme over any laws of convenience promoted by man supporting/honoring the little voice of evil within them. For thousands of years, the general consensus of civilized societies honored biblical laws against things like freedom of choice abortions, same-sex marriage, gambling, and the prostitution industry. Gradually, over the past century, these beliefs have been flipped to support what was outlawed before. Consider this statement from Romans 3:4: "Let God be true though Every Man a liar." *The war to destroy good common sense is crushing people's feeling of any worthwhile purpose.*

We have free will and can choose to do good and what's right or to do things we know are wrong. God has provided us with advice on how to live and act in peace toward all others. This book is not condemning anyone for the way they live and act, it only shares that advice along with examples of why we should want to follow our Creator's advice of our own free will.

Jesus Christ said He came to earth to save the lost sinners, not those who have judged themselves to be righteous. We are all sinners in need of Jesus Christ's gift of salvation. However, only those who are thankful for this gift will receive it. Only God and Jesus Christ know the persecution we are all suffering from Satan and his demonic angels at this time. Therefore, God said vengeance is His. It is not up to us to deal with evil because only He can ponder our hearts to know what our true character is really like.

Is it from persecution or through our own free will that we find ourselves doing evil things? The spirit of evil has no mechanical clout over us personally and cannot get physically involved. Instead, Satan's little voice must rely on convincing *us* to do evil. Mankind separated from the little voice of evil would act morally. We must always remember this. It is the reason our Father in heaven said we need to all love one another and be forgiving of each other's mistakes as we are reminded in the Lord's Prayer: *forgive us our trespasses as we forgive our trespassers.*

Regardless of how we perceive the actions of others, God Almighty wants us to love one another as God loves us.

The Age of Insanity

In 1968, I was in grade ten. We were shown some films on sexual diseases and the problem of unwanted babies conceived before their parents were mature married adults. Plus, we were instructed on the ill effects of taking drugs and how they damage all aspects of a person's life and the lives of their off-spring. At that time, hallucinogenic drugs were not available in my school, as far as I knew. And after considering the advice given, I had no desire to use drugs or even try them.

The next year, I started grade eleven in a newly built senior high school. Although drugs were still, to the best of my knowledge, not around at the beginning of the term, by the time school let out for the summer, it seemed about half of the students had begun to experiment with them. All of the students I had chummed with in junior high had deserted me as a friend because I would not take drugs.

By the end of grade twelve, everyone seemed to be doing drugs, and I ended up a loner, graduating without one close friend because I would not join in. They kept running me down as being a biased bigot. When I told them I had no desire to inject myself with an artificial personality, they would respond with the all-too-common "Hey, man, don't knock it if you haven't tried it, eh!"

I did not have to take drugs to see what they would do. I had a live experiment taking place right before my eyes each day at school, one I could observe with a sober, alert mind.

There were days when you could smell marijuana smoke in the corridors from all the pot being smoked in the cafeteria by students skipping classes. And this drug indulgence was the result of the madness of our society.

People are bound to become crazed when their little world is bombarded with despicable corruption caused by shameless greed of malevolent people who strive for power over others—malicious people who have zero concern for those they must hurt to get what they want.

In high school, staggering facts and statistics about evil events were thrown at us left, right, and center. It was enough to cause any student to flip out. We had been reared up in a fairy-tale dream world with mythical lies of heroes and magic presented as though they were reality. The world was dramatized as a place where everything is wonderful, where everyone good would be safe from tyrants and live happily ever after. In high school, we started to get a taste of the real world and sobered up to the realization that there are no visible or tangible heroes as portrayed in fairy tales.

Young people flip out when they learn about the true condition of the world: pollution, revolutions, and no visible solutions. When I was a student, we were taught that twenty-one thousand Americans became millionaires during the First World War as a result of the war. Was the war promoted to start a booming business? I don't know but the profitable results make you wonder. Also church leaders of the same faiths were blessing the men on both sides of the Second World War. Who was putting a gun to whose head to brainwash whom?

When we students related these facts to the senseless war in Vietnam, which was happening at that time, it left us numb. We saw live films shown on the news, daily, of little children being mowed down in hailstorms of bullets, in a war they claimed was required for reasons of economic necessity. All I could think of was, what's the use of growing up and having a family if this was the possible outcome to face any little ones I might have?

Banned songs spelling out the truth like "Eve of Destruction" (written by P. F. Sloan and sung by Barry McGuire) drove home the reality of what we were really growing up to face if we couldn't stop hating our neighbors.

I was confused as to who was who. When I watched people who called themselves peace-loving hippies cheering at the slaughter of women and children in a movie house, it left me dumfounded. That was the final blow. How madly insane had we become? Or had man always been this way?

The hippie belief was first started by a small group that called themselves "flower children." They said they were strictly for peace on earth between all mankind. However, like almost everything else on earth that becomes a fad, it became polluted with low moral characters—the beatniks of the fifties and other radicals. Almost overnight, the hippie fad included taking drugs, even drugging young girls and taking them to bed to express their favorite statement: "Make love, not war." However, what were they really doing?

- Producing unwanted fatherless children. *What type of lovemaking is that?*
- Spreading sexually transmitted disease worldwide. *What type of lovemaking is that?*
- Selling drugs to anyone, anywhere, and of any age they could entice to purchase their deadly merchandise and always at a high

profit to themselves. *Now really, what type of brotherly love is that?*

In my books, these were ruthless dealers who did not have any more concern for their fellow man than a hired killer. Their drug promotion propaganda included the suggestion: "Do your own thing." This encouraged stubborn, rebellious defiance. It promoted turning a deaf ear to any good moral advice from any source and instead laughing at moral wisdom as something from a former, now-discredited time. Old folks' advice was something that they said they did not need or want. The excuse they used to back up their reason to revolt was, "Look at the state of the world they have passed down to us."

Even our teachers were encouraging their students to be defiant to "do your own thing." The idea of listening to an old sage for wisdom was sneered at. And of course, the benevolent old sages are not the ones who caused the world to be in such a mess. It has always been the malevolent-minded people of all age groups who have caused things to be as bad as they are.

When the threat of AIDS was revealed, some wise people started trying to live by biblical moral instructions on sex. Some were concerned or scared enough that they started being very cautious about getting sexually involved before marriage. Many people were getting back to obeying the One who wanted men and women to enjoy clean and safe sexual intimacy— His wonderful gift of a sincere and honorable sexual relationship in a loving marriage, the proper way, as described in His written laws about sex and marriage in the Holy Bible. However, since we heard AIDS could be managed and is no longer a death sentence, morality has been traded for immorality once again.

Unfortunately, the fad of being stubborn and rebellious against responsible and good advice has caused many to destroy their own hopes for happiness from their youth onward. Youths who have been encouraged to distrust their parents and to rebel and ignore good advice end up in the clutches of those who lay snares for them, who prey on them, who strip them of their dignity, and leave them scarred with regret for the rest of their lives.

Some people, including some in government positions, try to fight against this evil business. However, the present dominant power of evil influences over everyone, particularly government leaders, prevents many of these attempts from being successful. Man's brainwashed society is gradually getting worse as Satan's time is coming to an end.

Since there is a god of evil, then it is a religion practiced by those who desire to, and believe in, and intend to do wicked deeds to increase their evilly acquired gains. The good spirit conscience inside these people warns them not to do wrong and they know better, but they go against nature's good advice and irresponsibly choose to side with the easy scheming ways they preferred to embrace.

Satan is very religion-oriented; his ethic is to enjoy doing anything whatsoever that goes against Jehovah God Almighty's responsible righteous laws of love. Satan wants you to prefer to live your life guided by his own unjust and defiant intentions of corrupt wickedness. It is an honorary salute to Satan when you willingly steal, lie, cheat, or exercise unnatural lusts with no concern for how it harms others mentally, physically, or socially.

Satan wants all of us, through any dishonest way we can, to willfully destroy nature to show our lack of respect for the world the happy God of love provided for us to live in. Isn't this why we see our governments back big businesses in their irresponsible destruction of the environment for big profits? Isn't this the prevailing way of man against his brethren in this dog-eat-dog world that Satan has cultivated? He plans to take everyone that he can with him into destruction.

You honor Satan when you use unrighteous man-made laws of convenience to divorce your family when you do not take responsible care of the gift of your family. This is written in 1 Timothy 5:8:

> But if any provide not for his own, and especially for those of his own house, he hath denied the faith, and is worse than an infidel.

If you abandon your spouse and/or your children for no valid reason other than personal lust, you truly have honored heathenism.

There are many other ways you can honor Satan's unrighteous defiance of the biblical laws of responsible and righteous living. Some of these are indulging in adultery, abortion, prostitution, or other lusts for unnatural sexual indulgence and any pagan rituals of satanic hatred worship, like the Ku Klux Klan, ISIS, or other hate groups. It doesn't matter which game you choose to start with, eventually with enough time spent at it, it is guaranteed that you will encompass all forms of evil.

We see it too often in the news. Someone meditates for days, months, even years about killing people at a school, home, social event, or place of business where they feel they were unjustly treated. They dwell on it continually, building up courage to execute their dastardly intentions. They know they're doing wrong because they try to prevent themselves from being detected before executing the act.

It is written: "Train a child in the way you want it to become when it grows up and it will not depart from it." Who can desire to live by Satan's disloyal, power-hungry, and immoral sexual ways today and expect to change his or her ways tomorrow? How can those who have chosen to program their mind to be a tyrannical beast today hope to become a meek, righteous, loving, and loyal person tomorrow? Who do you want to be adopted by in the end as your father, Jehovah God Almighty, or Satan, the devil?

No man, woman, or child is safe from the propaganda broadcast all over the earth in the form of violent immoral movies, fear-inducing propaganda, and other false teachings. This is gradualism propaganda from Satan's advocates, and its intent is to brainwash you to believe that the wickedness shown by the media should be your accepted way of life too. Satan is using his advocates in every way he can to try to crush your moral values.

Satan is determined to destroy the little voice of your good conscience so you cannot hear it any more.

Then he can totally possess your reasoning. Think about this: when you are having positive thoughts of doing good deeds, can't you sometimes feel a temptation force in your mind trying to urge you to dwell on the opposite thoughts of evil?

The Apostle Paul spoke of his frustration in dealing with evil temptations warring against his preferred righteous desires in Romans 7:18–25 and 8:1–2,

> For I know that in me [that is, in my flesh] dwelleth no good thing: for to will is present with me; but how to perform that which is good I find not.
>
> For the good that I would I do not: but the evil which I would not, that I do.
>
> Now if I do that I would not, it is no more I that do it, but sin that dwelleth in me.
>
> I find then a law, that, when I would do good, evil is present with me.
>
> For I delight in the law of God after the inward man:

But I see another law in my members, warring against the law of my mind, and bringing me into captivity to the law of sin which is in my members.

O wretched man that I am! Who shall deliver me from the body of this death?

I thank God through Jesus Christ our Lord. So then with the mind I myself serve the law of God; but with the flesh the law of sin.

There is therefore now no condemnation to them which are in Christ Jesus, who walk not after the flesh, but after the Spirit.

For the law of the Spirit of life in Christ Jesus hath made me free from the law of sin and death.

The good in us must contend with the evil in us. To have a hope of success at being a good person, we all must sober up (become alert); we need to become aware of the sly tricks Satan tempts us with. We need to sober up so we can truthfully examine the moral values we believe in—deep down inside us—and prefer to live by. We need to do this to clearly focus on the respect we need to have for ourselves and others. And we should do this on a regular basis because Satan is absolutely determined to never give up on pressuring us to dwell in his evil will. We should do this because that determines what we are worth to any relationship—in our family, with our neighbors, in business, and especially with our Creator.

Our Creator is observing our behavior to determine what we are. Therefore, do not let Satan's insanity rule you; guard yourself. Be loving, kind, and merciful toward all others. Jesus said at Matthew 25:40, "In-as-much as you have done it unto one of the least of these my brethren, you have done it unto me." Therefore, what are we doing to the One who died to save *all* of us from our sins when we exercise tyrant evils against children, women, or anyone else? When do you think it would be a good idea to get your house in order? Now? Or later, when it will be too late? Isn't it time to make amends by changing your ways for the future and praying for forgiveness? Learn about righteousness. Repent and be baptized as a believer in your heart and a lover of our Lord and Savior, Jesus Christ.

Ignore rebellious statements like, "Do your own thing," "Don't listen to those old fools," or "You are your own boss." Remember, these are statements to attack your better judgment. These are strategies used by Satan's advocates to sway your moral values to achieve his jealous plan to destroy your future. If anyone tries to entice you with one of these attack statements, do not reply, just walk away. Do not argue with them. They seek to destroy you by trapping you in their language addictions to inhibit your moral reasoning by basically ambushing your mind. The most powerful statement you can make against their attack statements is to walk away from them. Period. Why would you willingly battle with the devil on his terms?

None of us must indulge personally in anything that we have been warned is bad before we have the right to reject it as bad for us. Remember it's the same old deceitful lying trick that Satan played on Eve in the garden of Eden. Do what is right even if you must do it alone. If you go about your life in this righteous way, then your Father in heaven, Jehovah God Almighty, will be exceedingly pleased with your wise decision. And He will reward you in the end for loving Him and His righteousness instead of Satan.

There are times when personal troubles have us depressed to the point of exhaustion. In these times, we are attacked in another way. Often at these times, we are challenged by the tempting victory chant of

Satan's insanity: "If you can't beat them, join them." Do not let yourself be lured into this subtle trap. It is a short-lived feeling of vengeance against our fear of failure, and it will become a grave mistake to engage in this type of thinking. If you give in, you will have ignored your own good common sense to partner with evil. Some who consent to this unrighteousness for a short while survive, but many are scarred for life or destroyed in some way, waking up only when it is already too late to avoid suffering the consequences for having abandoned their moral conscience.

As a typical example of how this scars people who believe in living by righteous ways, think of how you feel when you see your peers having an enjoyable time doing something you know is wrong. You feel alone because you won't go along with it. Perhaps nobody will associate with you because you refuse to join in. Your choices are to stand alone for what you believe or to give in to the temptation and go along with them for friendship's sake. Remember this promise at Matthew 5:5 from Jesus Christ to us when evil temptation challenges you:

> Blessed are the meek, for they
> shall inherit the earth.

A meek person is not a weak person. *A meek person is one who has power under control.* It is a lot easier to follow the crowd or gang going the wrong way than to stand alone for what is right. To stand alone takes real stamina and a strong determined spirit for what is good. In this context, meek definitely is not weak.

On the other hand, the bullies, cowards, and yes-people who hide in crowds and fear what others will think of them if they don't go with the gang's ways are very weak. They are more concerned about being accepted by degenerate gangs than by God Almighty.

Lack of Guidance

The insanity of those who are blinded by corrupt influences is everywhere. Laws have been put in force to stop parents from having any assertive correction for their children. When a child does wrong, man's law now says they can't be corrected by corporal punishment—no matter how far the situation gets out of hand. Even if your child intentionally inflicts serious injury on another, your only recourse is to tell them not to do it again. How is anyone with an aggressive nature going to learn anything from this type of passive and soft-spoken correction? It is no more effective than blowing on a bonfire to put it out.

For sociologists, teachers, and the laws of society to insist that violent children must not be corrected by any form of corporal punishment is utter madness. The Bible talks about atheists who profess to be wise in Romans 1:21–22,

> Although they knew God, they neither glorified him as God nor gave thanks to him, but their thinking became futile and their foolish hearts were darkened.
> Professing to be wise, they became fools.

The laws around child abuse have gone way overboard, leading to very defiant youth. Who can be raised without paying the consequences for being unruly? How can the experts expect these unruly children to develop good and mature judgment when they have grown up without consequences? The only thing they will have learned is to disrespect any form of authority, law, and order.

Punishment for a youth involved with stealing or malicious damage to property consists of telling the youth that they have done a naughty thing, and that they should quit doing it. Police are handicapped until the youth comes of age for adult court and goes out again and does something criminal. They are old enough to know the consequences, but they have never experienced the consequences of anything bad they have done before, and now this person is liable for punishment to the full extent of the law. Society outlawed discipline when it could have had a beneficial effect for this youth, and now it is too late.

Discipline should start in the high chair, not the electric chair.

Proper Discipline

Beating a child and causing bodily damage is absolutely child abuse but a proper spanking when required is not. I believe in following the steps I have listed below in chastising a child who is misbehaving:

First you must be a good example for them to look up to. That means you must be an honest and sincere parent worthy of respect. You must be a disciplined disciplinarian, living by the good citizen ways you're trying to teach your child to follow. You must be gentle when you can be and firm when you have to be. This attitude in a parent often gains them the respect of their children to the point that their child may never need a spanking.

However, not everybody has the same character. There are some situations you can work through with lectures and restitution more than others. When a child insists on being a bully, or they haven't heeded their first warning about playing with something, like matches, then it is a serious matter that requires the corporal punishment of a sound spanking.

Sociologists, teachers, and the law society should not rebuke sincere and loving parents for spanking their child over serious matters like playing with matches or bullying. A parent should also never walk away after having administered a spanking to their children but should talk about what happened that left you, as a responsible parent, with no other choice. Let them know you love them. If you truly are a disciplined disciplinarian, their respect and love for you will grow stronger and stronger as they grow up.

Today, some police departments are pleading for parents to spank their kids when required. We have far too many youth who are arrogant, disrespectful, and unruly with no common sense reasoning or respect for law and order. This has gotten so far out of hand because too many parents have stopped using any form of punishment; they have been taught and believe it is wrong.

At my junior high school, shortly after corporal punishment was outlawed in the early 1970s, the students held a vote to find out whether or not they wanted the strap back in school or not for misbehaving students. The newspaper stated that the clear majority voted that they would like to see it put back in use, and students gave a couple of practical reasons for their opinion:

- With no effective discipline, class disruption was affecting everyone who wanted to learn.
- They said they felt a deep sense of insecurity among the students because there was no effective form of punishment to deter bullies, and fear was affecting some students' ability to learn.

What these students had to say was practical common sense but was totally ignored by the system.

In around 1989–90, our son was in grade five. He was being bullied by a bigger boy who was systematically inflicting such painful bodily injury that our son missed school for days on several occasions. In one episode, the bully punched our son so hard in the stomach that school staff had to take him to the hospital. The only disciplinary action was another suspension from attending school for a few days. Of course, this was nothing but pure encouragement to get out of having to go to school. The discipline he got was the reward he desired.

My wife and I were not successful asking school staff to deal with this in an effective manner and ended up complaining to the head of the school board. We went to the school board office. They had no intention of doing anything about it either and instead suggested we hire a lawyer. They might as well display a sign advertising that the bullying of innocent children is tolerated here, but corporal punishment against such bullies is against school policy because it might violate the bullies' rights.

Lack of proper discipline has proven beneficial for Satan's unrighteous lawlessness, permeating every segment of human society. Parents are afraid for their children to play outside because of child molesters, who hardly get a slap on the wrist for their disgusting deeds. Students are afraid of becoming victims of bullies with no recourse. In many municipalities, even grown people are now afraid to just go for a walk down the street for recreational exercise because of the villains who prey on people.

My grandmother told me that around 1900, a man in Oklahoma was brought up on charges for beating his wife. He claimed he had lost his mind and was sentenced to thirty days in jail. Shortly after his release, he beat his wife again, claiming again that he had lost his mind. Jailing him hadn't worked to prevent a second attack, so this time, he received ten lashes with a bullwhip. My grandmother said that man never lost his mind again. Bullies get the message when their hide pays the price.

Background studies on the family history of criminals have shown that violent offenders come from families where *proper* discipline was not exercised. The more negligence there was toward enforcing *responsible* discipline, the more violent and insensitive the criminals were found to become.

A few years ago, I went back to my hometown to visit an old friend. We got on the subject of some naughty things we did as young rascals, and we had a whale of a good time laughing about the spankings we used to get and discussing the different tactics we tried to use to get out of receiving some of those lickings that we knew full well we deserved. More than thirty-five years later, we were laughing so hard about the corporal punishment we received as kids that tears were rolling down our faces.

We knew our parents loved us and were only interested in getting us on the right track. We did not resent our parents for trying to correct us. All I can remember over the years as I meditate on various aspects of life is how thankful I am that they did what they could to get my mind right when I was young. I cannot understand where philosophers got the idea that corporal punishment in the form of a *proper* spanking will emotionally damage our children.

In the Book of Proverbs, God states that if we, as parents, do not admonish our children—discipline them—then we hate them. (Rather than quoting chapter and verse here, I'll use this opportunity to recommend you read the Book of Proverbs for yourself. It is full of good priceless advice.)

Society has rejected spanking as destructive to a child's morale. I grew up with parents whom, without a doubt, I knew loved me. This is not the case with children in the care of strangers, for example, foster care. Therefore, I needed to learn what the terms in the Holy Bible really mean about the rod of correction. Statements like "Withhold not correction from the child: for if thou beat him with the 'rod' (advice) he shall not die" (Proverbs 23:13) and "*Chasten* thy son while there is still hope, and let not thy soul spare for his crying" (Proverbs 19:18). Sounds like spankings are the answer to misbehavior until you look deeper.

Comparing all Bible verses with the words *rod* and *staff* in them, I found the word *rod* stands for "advice taken whether it is good or bad," and the word *staff* refers to "the mentor or advisor you look up to (faithfully respect)." As such, the statement, "Don't be an undisciplined disciplinarian" is the most important concern in disciplining children because the way you carry yourself will have the greatest influence on the way they will become in the end. For it says, "Train up a child in the way he should go: and when he is old, he will not depart from it" (Proverbs 22:6). Therefore, the most important discipline you need to take care of is your own by ending personal bad habits and not being a hypocrite.

Just the Right Medicine

Sometimes, we feel it is too late to have any effective way to get a child's mind right on how they should live their life. My wife and I provided foster care for a fifteen-year-old who was totally out of control in grade ten but reading at a grade three level. One day, we put on a movie for him to watch, *To Sir, With Love*, with Sidney Poitier as a new teacher saddled with the job of schooling a class of out-of-control and poorly educated teens in their final year of school.

By the time the movie was over, our foster child was so impressed with its message that he made it his business to watch it over and over and over again. It became an almost-daily obsession. Two years later, he graduated from high school with honors.

We never know what medicine might be required to get the message across and help others become mature adults, but for anything to work, we who are doing the rearing must conduct ourselves morally as disciplined disciplinarians.

Misappropriating God's Word

In Sunday school, I was taught that when we did something wrong, all we had to do was say, "sorry" and all was forgiven by God. I noticed kids being mean to others and immediately saying, "I'm sorry." The assumption was this quick, hollow apology kept them in good standing with God and meant no one could retaliate. In other words, it was their license to get away with anything.

Years later, after I'd moved to a new town, I was invited to go to a church youth group. They were teaching the same message: if you do anything wrong, ask God to forgive you, and all will be forgiven. What they weren't teaching was that *God ponders your heart for what your intentions really are* (Proverbs 21:2). In Matthew 15:8–9, God says, "You worship me with your mouth, but your heart is far from me."

Now, fifty years later, it seems nothing has changed. I recently overheard a nine-year-old boy being mean to his little sister and to others, saying he was sorry each time. When another child told him what he was doing was ungodly, the bully replied, "God will always forgive you as long as you say you are sorry." If no one corrects his thinking on this, what kind of adult will he grow up to be?

Some people grow up to become coldhearted business criminals because they were not exposed to sharing and caring as children. These days, it is becoming increasingly hard to know what or who can be trusted. And some people cleverly use isolated biblical quotes to steer you wrong without revealing to you the big picture of what they actually want you to do for them.

In 1977, I met a man who was using this technique to run a business selling fire alarms. While recruiting and in training sessions, he held up the Bible and kept saying, "We were saving lives," using a sermon to whip his salesmen into shape to go out and sell as many fire alarms as we could. Convinced that I would be doing a good deed for people, I quit a well-paid job to work for him.

I was zealous about trying to sell the alarms, although I couldn't bring myself to be as aggressive as he had tried to teach us to be. People in the small community I was living in took a liking for me, and after about three weeks of going door to door selling the alarms, some strangers asked if I would come by their home to give them a presentation. I was selling more alarms than all the other salesmen combined who were working in the larger center about a hundred miles away. However, the head of the company was so cheap with commissions that I still had to take money out of my bank account to add to my wages to live. I was debt-free, I was single, and I was living by simple means; but I still had to subsidize my income with my banked savings. It was much worse for one of the other salesmen who had a wife and little ones to care for.

One day, about a month after I started selling, I knocked on the door of a person who had just bought a fire alarm via mail order. To my surprise, it was exactly the same as the one we were selling. She got hers for $50. We were selling them for $128 each and getting only $10 commission for each alarm we sold. Clearly, I had been used. And how many innocent trusting customers had I ripped off? In my books, we had been tricked to work as hired thieves. Our boss had used his bible to gain our trust and convinced us we were saving lives when really we were using scare tactics to drain people's wallets for him. Before I quit, I told him what I had learned. He immediately offered to triple my commission from $10 to $30 per alarm. I said forget it and went on with my life.

Many a time, even with the desire to want to do good, we are blinded by those who use us to do wrong. The owner of that business was like many other people who proclaim to be God-fearing, righteous leaders but are really wolves in sheep's clothing. The Holy Bible warns us about these people in plenty of scriptures such as 1 John 4:1, which says, "Beloved, believe not every spirit, but try the spirits whether they are of God: because many false prophets are gone into the world."

Satan's advocates are always trying to do anything they can to tempt unrighteous, wicked people to deceive others. Demon-possessed men often use religious scriptures in twisted ways to keep humble people from learning that they are being tricked and enslaved by the devil's wickedness.

I found something I can trust, and that helps me to be free from stress even under heavy persecution.

That is personally reading the living Word of Almighty God in the Holy Bible for understanding and advice, especially when in a lot of trouble. Then I compare its advice to the advice I see many people following today. There are good and bad spiritual and political leaders, so you must be shrewd, letting God's Word be your decisive authority on every matter.

It is important for you to read the Holy Bible for yourself rather than let others read and interpret it for you; they can steer you wrong. Those who love our Lord and Savior but rely solely on their leaders instead of reading the Holy Bible themselves are flying blindfolded.

Historically, Nazis presented Jesus Christ as favoring their "pure" race to motivate people to war against other countries. The words of the Holy Bible have been twisted to justify slavery, and today the Ku Klux Klan still uses the Holy Bible in twisted ways to promote hatred. No true Christian harbors any hatred against any man of any status or race. Period. They understand the consequences of hating anyone, as is stated in 1 John 3:14, "We know that we have passed from death unto life, because we love the brethren. He that loveth not his brother abideth in death."

You need not ever be a slave to any man-promoted idea that dictates anything outside of God's love. We need only honor our Father in heaven, who created us and gave us His living Word for guidance in the Holy Bible.

Intoxicants and Altered Reality

Before I really found something I could trust, I reached a point in my life where all the insanity I saw going on broke my spirit; I lost hope for any good for the future on this earth and had no desire to go on living. Hate built up inside me for what I saw: billions being spent on warfare, while farmers were denied a fair return on their labor. Watergate. The Vietnam War. Everybody seemed to be like blind fools, accepting and following the examples set by criminally minded leaders in all forms of leadership roles. I observed leaders preaching patriotism and good moral values while showing they had none of their own. I allowed myself to focus on all of the unrighteousness I saw and the bitterness I felt toward it, blinding myself to any righteous reasoning.

In a rage of hate for the way I felt, I turned to alcohol and used it as my mind-altering drug of choice. This happened before I finished school, and it turned out to be all I needed to condition myself to thinking about indulging in criminal activities. My intention was to try to forget about the madness of the world's immoral ways, but instead alcohol amplified my anguish, and that turned my reasoning to another type of out. I had poisoned my body so I couldn't hear my good conscience and went through a series of steps down the wrong path. Eventually, I considered it reasonable to get involved in a Robin Hood type of career. It made good sense to me to steal from the rich since, I reasoned, many of them steal from the poor. Before I knew it, I'd become a common thief.

I got involved in insurance fraud. But I justified it in my mind. We were barely scraping by when my mother shared her dismay that a magazine was offering President Nixon a million dollars for an interview on how he pulled off the Watergate scandal. So if a man of his wealth and power was offered a million-dollar reward for his wrongdoing, how could there be anything wrong with someone poor stealing from wealthy insurance companies?

When people are poor and they see all the lavish waste of money by governments, it can enrage any one of us to revolt against that type of society. All rebellions, including major ones like the Russian, French, and American Revolutions, start from rebellion against the wickedness that has caused the poor to suffer intolerable burdens while the wealthy live in luxury and benefit at the expense of others.

I did not have a sound understanding of our Creator's solution when scheming my own small rebellion. And I did not realize at the time that I was actually causing an increased burden against the poor, not against the rich. Satan had blinded me, steered me to do injury to my brethren. I am glad I was caught before my situation got too far out of hand.

On June 13, 1971, I spent the day in jail, being interrogated several times while an investigation took place. But I refused to talk. Then when meals were to be served, the guard asked us in the jail cells to pray. I do not know what anyone else did in the other cells, but I did pray. Right away, I was taken out of the cell for another interrogation. However, this time, it was more of a good common sense talking to. The RCMP officer said, "Look, why don't you admit to what you have done, and get this problem off your chest. Otherwise, this will haunt you for the rest of your life until we do have enough evidence to convict you. Your parents have been down here to see about you twice already today, and from what I have seen of them, they are concerned people who tried to raise you to be a decent, honest citizen."

He could not have said truer words. My eyes felt like fire from smarting, and I broke down crying bitterly with shame for what I had become. The officer was right; it was time to clean the slate, pay my debt to society no matter what it was, and get on with my life. Some governing leaders are corrupt, but this is no reason for us to practice being the same.

A few days later, I went to my high school graduation, believing that I would have to do two or three years behind bars once the court case was over. When I got three years' probation and had to pay $4,600 in restitution, I was extremely grateful that I did not have to spend another minute in jail.

I overheard other people in the courtroom who were waiting to hear their cases, muttering that the judge had been very hard on me to make me pay out so much money rather than spend some time in jail. At that time, the average adult in a good-paying industrial job earned about $3,500 annually before taxes. Paying restitution demanded a lot of responsibility and was far more worthwhile to me than spending time in a bad environment. The one day I spent in jail listening to others dwelling on their own hatred and wrongdoing had already helped me realize that my grandmother was right when she said, "The idle mind is the devil's workshop."

After I finished school, I started a landscaping business. I worked hard to do a quality job for my customers; and by the time my probation was finished, I had become well-known and liked for being an honest, fair contractor. However, I shudder to think what I could have become. In such a short time, I had swung so far from what I had *known* was right growing up. Who is safe?

Try your best to do what is morally decent no matter what the rest of the world is doing. Don't let the insanity of evil rule you. This is vitally important because if you give in to listening to Satan and his advocates, you will have allowed bad judgment to control your life. Be aware that the ignorance of hatred and jealousy can, like any mind-altering drug, poison your reasoning and allow an artificial personality to rule you.

Fostering Disrespect of Oneself and Others

One typical example of a disgusting leader is a father who teaches his sons (by intention or through suggestion or example) that it is all right to use girls as casual sex toys. Sometimes, these same fathers have totally different expectations for their daughters.

Women, just like men, need a passionate relationship with someone they feel they can trust as a sincere friend. For such relationships to be proper and right, every passionate relationship should be a sacred one between one man and one woman.

By law, buggery in many parts of the world was once punishable by the death sentence. No questions asked. Buggery laws were relaxed in the late sixties in Canada, England, and West Germany followed by many other countries gradually decriminalizing it. In the 1970s, they turned a blind eye to pornographic magazines strongly promoting indulgence in homosexual relationships and group orgies. In the 1980s, the American medical community grappled with a sudden spike in rare types of pneumonia, cancer, and other illnesses primarily among actively homosexual men. Because these conditions were uncommon in people with healthy immune systems, public health officials used the term *acquired immunodeficiency syndrome* or AIDS. Eventually the source was traced to a virus, HIV, almost identical to the SIV virus found in a particular subspecies of African chimpanzees.

Regardless of its origins, the virus spreads through contact with infected blood, which is a frequent occurrence during homosexual activity. God did not design the rectum to cope with the vigorous activity of sexual intercourse, which the female's vagina is designed for. When a male allows another male to use their rectum for sexual gratification, they can end up with a ruptured colon membrane of the large intestine, allowing dangerous bacteria into the bloodstream.

Did the Holy Bible warn us of the danger? I found what I think is the most reasonable answer in the Holy Bible in Romans 1:24–27:

> Therefore, God also gave them up to uncleanness in the lusts of their hearts, to dishonor their bodies among themselves, who exchange the truth of God for the lie and worshipped and served the creature [Satan] rather than the Creator [God], who is blessed forever. Amen.
>
> For this reason, God gave them up to vile passions. For even their women exchanged the natural use for what is against nature;
>
> Likewise, also the men leaving the natural use of the woman, burned in their lust for one another, men with men committing what is

shameful, and receiving in themselves the penalty of their error
(AIDS) which was due.

AIDS/HIV also spreads more quickly among people who used intravenous drugs. How far wrong can we
be led by listening to the bad little voice of evil spirit
in us, along with the shrewdness of those already committed to a defiant nature against our Creator? The sly
influences of demonic spirits start out as a spark that
can quickly get out of hand, becoming a raging forest
fire if you decide to gravitate toward it. Drugs can cause
a transition from a good nature to a bad one very rapidly before you realize what you have become.

Our Lord and Savior, Jesus Christ, knew from
experience the curses that we deal with under Satan's
demonic influence over mankind. While Jesus was on
earth, he expelled demons from people possessed by
them by his authoritative word—by ordering them
out of people. He came to earth from God to live the
only totally righteous life to be lived by a man born of
flesh and blood. Therefore, He allowed His blood to be
shed for our sins to be pardoned from us if we choose
to accept His gift. Jesus Christ's sacrificial gift was not
for some but for everyone because He loves every one
of us. If He didn't, He would not have said what He did

just before He died the horrendous crucifixion death on the cross: "Forgive them Father for they know not what they do."

I was blinded with hatred and ignorance when I got in trouble with the law. I did not wake up from the criminal state I had embraced until I was told by the police the truth of what my parents had tried to raise me to be. I have seen too many others in similar and other ways become swayed just as fast, so it is easy for me to see why Jesus said, "Forgive them Father for they know not what they do."

However, this does not protect those who hate being corrected. The New Testament is about Jesus Christ coming to earth to save sinners. Therefore, since we all are sinners, we need to pay attention to 1 Corinthians 6:9–11. It indicates that if you turn away from doing wrong, you will be forgiven by our Lord Jesus Christ. We must always remember: *we can look at these scriptures that show God's teachings, but we personally cannot judge anyone.*

God Almighty states that vengeance is His and His alone because only He can ponder our hearts. We cannot dictate what caused anyone to become the way they are. Only God Almighty can determine whether anything was of an individual's intended will or the result of them being oppressed and tricked by evil spirits to end up doing what they do.

There is no end to the wickedness that the flesh will aspire to if it stops paying attention to the good little spirit of goodness in you.

The Spoils of War

During the First World War, millions of people went to the slaughter while millionaires on all sides of the conflict became wealthier. Then they did it again in the Second World War because people still trusted in them. When they started the Vietnam War, the youth of the world ended up rebelling against it. However, it did not end there. If you ever want to know what is going on, all you need to do is follow the money. Wealth is not evil of itself but the decision to gain wealth by unrighteous means is.

King Solomon, the wealthiest person who ever lived, asked only to be blessed with wisdom. God was pleased with his request and gave it to him. Thus, he became not only the wisest man but also the richest man who ever existed. Solomon's reign was also the longest period in history of world peace. One of the reasons for this was that he ruled with justice and was fair to everyone. He did not tolerate corruption designed to support business theft. He did not support a system that helped enrich lawyers by focusing on harsh penalties for criminals while overlooking the needs of their victims or one that enriched doctors and psychiatrists by relaxing abortion laws. He did not tolerate practices that today are making hundreds of millions of dollars for doctors treating AIDS outbreaks all over the world.

Can you see how corrupt laws are big money makers for professionals all at the expense of the poor? When I consider the merciful blessings Jesus was doing healing people, I can easily see why the professional scribes and Pharisees planned His cruel death. He was destroying their wicked business of preying on innocent victims of poor health.

Think about the laws of convenient divorce, which are most painful for the innocent children caught in the middle. Who stands to benefit? Divorce is another practice that is making millions of dollars for lawyers, doctors, and psychiatrists, etc.

The book *7 Steps to Health* by Max Sidorov KN reveals over a hundred years of health benefits destroyed and suppressed from the public by the modern scribes and Pharisees, conspiracies to destroy our health to make themselves rich. It exposes the cleverly engineered lies to make and keep you sick until they have wrung every cent they can out of you. It also describes in depth nature's health benefits we can use instead to avoid their expensive toxic brews. After reading this book, I asked myself: Is there anything left that is not polluted with deceptive and monstrous lies?

Cults

Since the Dark Ages, religious cults have become more subtle. Back then, they publicly burned people at the stake for reading the Holy Bible or even so much as having one in their possession. Why? It's the book that teaches that we need not be a slave to any man.

The more anyone tries to lord themselves over others, and the more their slaves prefer to be a part of the gang, the more unrighteous, hardened, and wicked they all become. The leaders and the followers feed off the loyal support of each other, and the results are situations like the Jonestown massacre and Waco Texas.

The witchcraft and wizardry of gradualism works like a spark that flares up and becomes as a raging forest fire that's totally out of control. Have you met someone whom you have tried to give good advice to but found that they totally block you out as though they have become possessed? People who are defiant against what they know to be true about God Almighty become psychologically sick. Consider this quote from the Jerusalem Bible, Romans 1:28:

> In other words, since they refused to see it was rational to acknowledge God, God has left them to their own irrational ideas and to their monstrous behavior.

It does not say they *may* become sick, it says they *become* mentally sick. It is scary to think that anyone who delves into unrighteousness and expresses no remorse afterward is possessed with evil spirits that have taken control of them. The New Testament clearly describes the existence of demons taking control of people. Up until Jesus started casting out demons from people, nobody knew it was possible.

In how many ways can you be misled if the head people in a church you attend are possessed by demons? Your best safeguard is to read the Holy Bible for yourself and insist on scripture to back any demands made on you by the head people of the church. The New Testament of the Holy Bible gives all kinds of warnings about false churches and phony priests.

The Holy Bible makes it clear that we do not have to be under subjection to anyone else. It states in many places that Jehovah God intentionally made us and all the angels with our own free spirit to do the will of our hearts.

Back in 1976, I drove a friend and his girlfriend over to a woman's home in Prince George so she could get paid for babysitting. We were invited in for a coffee, and while we were visiting, a teenager stopped by to collect her babysitting pay too. When she joined the conversation, I heard firsthand about her near miss with a cult.

She told us she had been instructed under hypnosis to go to Vancouver, British Columbia, to a certain place to be used as a sacrifice. But the transit system that she had been instructed to use had changed the bus routes, so she stood at a bus stop for several hours waiting for a bus that never came. The Vancouver city police noticed and recognized her as a missing child from Prince George. She wanted nothing more to do with the church, but the minister was demanding she continue attending. I explained that God gave us our own free will to go to church or not as we pleased. She felt very relieved and quit going.

A couple of days later, I was talking to my mother's next-door neighbor about what I'd heard about that teenager's situation and found out that his business partner was the father of that girl. All that I had heard was absolutely true.

The following spring, an RCMP officer knocked on my apartment door in Fort St. James. He asked me where I was on a certain day about six weeks earlier. I asked him to come in, and we went to my calendar to try to figure it out. At that time, I worked shifts in Fort St. James and spent most of my days off back in Prince George. On that particular Sunday, I was working day shift as the boiler operator. He asked me if I was sure. I said yes and that it would be recorded in the company's logbook. Then I asked him what was going on, and he told me I had been accused of burning down a church in Prince George that Sunday afternoon—obviously an impossibility, since I was at work a hundred miles away. It was the same cult church the teenage girl had quit.

When I got back to Prince George, I learned that the minister of that church ran into the girl on the street not long before the church was burned down and gave her hell for not attending his cult. She told him God gave us free will, and when he demanded she tell him where she had heard this, she told him about me.

Apparently, the church had been set on fire twice. The first fire was quickly put out, but in the early afternoon, it caught fire again, and the building burned to the ground. The minister of the church told the police I had done it, but after the police talked to me, they investigated the minister and discovered he was wanted for burning several churches in the United States.

Most churches are good churches that believe in teaching the truth about the Bible and God Almighty. However, there are some crazed demonic cults out there that we all must be cautious of getting involved with. So if your children start going to a church you are unfamiliar with, then go to it yourself to see what they are getting into. Do you see a good mixture of people of all age groups, or is it way out of balance with a large majority of young or old people? Churches should be very family-oriented. Another lack of balance is if it is all children and mothers with basically no fathers. Also check the history of the church. On what was it founded?

I was asked by one religion to read the scriptural book that they said was additional found scripture of the Holy Bible. I was a young Christian then, but I knew about the warning in Revelations against anything being added to the living Word of the Holy

Bible. Still, they duped me into promising to read it. I prayed to God about it, and then let their book fall open, focusing on the page. I read one paragraph and slammed the book shut, shocked. I let the book fall open again, about a hundred pages from the first reading, and tried again. Just as shocked as before, I decided I was finished reading the book.

The next time I saw these people, they wanted to know if I had read their book. I told them the language seemed Shakespearean to me, and they agreed with me that it was. If those were supposed to be ancient scriptures, then why wasn't the book written in the style of Jesus Christ's time on earth? I'd also learned a couple of other bizarre things about that church's history that did not synchronize with the nature of God's loving way.

The Holy Bible warns against those who claim to be Christ Himself, and it also strongly urges us to become personally familiar with the teaching of its scriptures by reading through them ourselves.

What were some churches in the Dark Ages doing when they sentenced anyone they caught read or even so much as possessing a copy of the Holy Bible to execution? There is a statement written in the Holy Bible at Jeremiah 17:5 about trusting in another person to

show you the truth instead of doing the research work
for yourself:

> Thus, saith the Lord; Cursed
> be the man that trust in man, and
> make flesh his arm and whose heart
> departeth from the Lord.

The more you know about the living Word of God
in the Holy Bible, the more knowledge you have to protect yourself from any cult business.

One church that I checked out was really into the
belief that they alone were the only way to meet with
God's approval. Then one day in church, they got into
chanting the name of the man who founded that religion. We are to worship only our Creator, Jehovah God
Almighty and His only begotten Son who is our Lord
and Savior, Jesus Christ. Chanting is praising (glorify-
ing); therefore, I walked out of there, never to return.

A lot of nice people go to that church, and I don't
mind talking to them about scripture. However, they
seem to be in a trance because anything you find
that runs contrary to what they have been taught to
believe, no matter how plain the language is, they
insist that you are absolutely wrong and they are

absolutely right. Therefore, my word of advice to you is, don't go to church blind.

A coworker of mine gave me the book *In God's Name* by David A. Yallop about corrupt powers in some churches. I only read the first thirty or so pages of it and gave it back. The book documents the work of power-hungry mobsters who arranged the murder of anyone who became a threat to their corruption. It clearly shows that there are rulers in the world today who do not follow the teachings of Jehovah God and instead use their churches for wrong.

By the time I was twenty-six, I had met and had dealt with some people proclaiming to be religious, God-fearing people through my landscaping business. The sad thing is, I found more of them were a problem to collect payment from than people who proclaimed to be atheists. It ended up happening so often that I became very leery when prospective clients introduced themselves as God-fearing Christians. Eventually, when I learned I was dealing with another religious person, it caused me to be on guard. Even though I have always been a believer in the existence of a righteous and Almighty loving God of the universe and His only begotten Son, Jesus Christ of Nazareth, as my Lord and Savior, I became extra cautious of anyone who said they were the same—a Christian. It's sad but in the New Testament, there are many warnings about ravenous wolves in sheep's clothing, posing as shepherds of Christian faith. It is little wonder why people say they do not believe in a God of good when those proclaiming to be God-fearing people do wrong. It is little wonder why some people refuse to go to church, stating it is full of hypocrites.

Some people are so bitter about the detestable conditions on this earth today that they say a God of goodness cannot exist. If such a God were to exist, they ask, then why has He allowed this earth to become as it is, full of war, starvation, and injustice? "If an Almighty God does exist and has allowed all this suffering, especially the suffering of innocent little children, I do not want to have anything to do with him."

Well, that is a tough argument, and it had me puzzled for a time. I now understand the bad things have to do with the challenge of free choice, allowing us to freely choose for ourselves whether we will honor Jehovah God Almighty or Satan, the devil.

The End of the Age of Insanity

I also discovered plenty of sound reasons to support biblical prophecies of the future to come, prophecies that promise to wipe away every tear permanently after this time of Satan is over. For me, it was a big relief to find logical realities that resolved my concerns about separating what is true from what is false. I have always been a seeker of undisputable facts on which to base my understanding about anything.

When we look at the unspoiled wilderness in nature and consider the delicate balance of everything to support life on this planet, it reveals strong evidence of a passionate and loving designer whose intentions were for a paradise earth. The Holy Bible clearly shows the difference between the Creator's good intentions for the earth and Satan's destructive intentions against anything good. Lucifer figured because of his beauty, he was better than God. He became puffed up with pride about himself and said that if given the chance, he would prove that man would rather worship him than God, just as Adam and Eve were conned into doing. And because our Creator, God Almighty, is not an oppressor, He has given Lucifer the opportunity to prove his point once and for all for all time to come.

It grieves our Creator to see us suffering as we are. And He promises that all this suffering will end, and those who love righteousness will be resurrected to a second life in a paradise world even better than it was in the garden of Eden. Therefore, God changed the name of the creator of lies, who was Lucifer, to Satan, the insane father of lies.

Today, we are living in the very last days of the time allotted for Satan to prove his point. Satan knows his time is short. And in his anger, he is doing everything he can to get as many people as he can to blindly follow his evil ways. He is accomplishing his strategy by diverting our attention away from the logic of the happy God of love.

Civilization had at least five thousand years of recorded history with almost no new development in technology. Then within a few decades of the last century, man went from the horse-and-buggy era to the space age. The telephone has only been around for a little over one hundred years, and look at the advancements in them. Today anyone can send a message to anyone anywhere on earth in an instant.

The Book of Daniel, written over three thousand years ago, states that knowledge would increase expeditiously in the last days. "But thou, O Daniel, shut up the words and seal the book, even to the time of the time of the end: many shall run to and fro, and knowledge shall be increased."

How much do we have available today to distract our attention away from the basic logical fundamentals of life? Many people spend their whole day glued to their cell phones. What is Satan preparing people for?

The gradual accelerating transformation into the cyberspace age has produced mindless zombies transfixed by the Internet. I was on a bus a few years ago when a middle-aged man engrossed with his phone stepped out in front of us. The bus had to brake hard and managed to stop only a couple of feet from him, but the man didn't seem to notice; he simply continued texting as he finished crossing the street. That man is only one of millions of people so immersed in their cell phone or iPad that they are totally out of touch with the reality around them.

Drinking and driving was once the number one cause of deadly accidents. Now it's from people texting while driving. Oh my, how Satan has desensitized man's reasoning with the electronic age. Very few people today take the time to sit quietly and ponder; they just go with the flow of whatever society says we should think. Who do you think is controlling this?

Man's moral way of thinking has changed drastically in the past century. Who has been behind this? And what's their motive? Down through history, evildoers have forever diverted focus away from what they really are to what they want the public to believe they are. They are, as I said earlier, salesmen convincing you to go to hell in such a way that you will be looking forward to the trip.

Judge Not

There is nothing wrong with hating evil that we see being done by others, *but it is not right to hate people for doing evil.* The higher the position is that anyone trying to do good have over other people, the more Satan puts persecution on them to spearhead corruption. Therefore, it takes a powerful moral leader who puts all his faith and love in Jesus Christ to be victorious over this evil. Also, none of us can know how the people we see doing evil would be if they were raised up in a different situation. However, there is one thing we do know; that is, all of us are sinners. Therefore, Jesus said, "Let he who is without sin cast the first stone" (John 8:7).

Hating political leaders is allowing yourself to get sidetracked. Any hate you feel for what is wrong should only be directed at Satan, the devil, and his demonic angels. God says for us to pray for our fellow man and for our governments to do that which is righteous and good. With concerns like COVID-19, all governments worldwide need our prayers to do what is best for us all.

One place Satan gets the better of us is through bribes. Who among us, if we were in a government position, would not find ourselves tempted by unrighteous lobbyist bribers? It takes a man or woman who is determined in their mind to walk tall for righteousness' sake. No matter how hard any of us have tried to live by this moral way, all of us have failed at it to some degree. So who of us can be the true judge? Only God Almighty.

Another place Satan gets the better of us is when we watch the news. We see many stories about bad things that have been done. When criminals have been caught, they give the names of the people charged and convicted of the crimes. Often, we feel a rage of hatred against whoever did the crime. This is exactly what Satan wants you to feel because it goes against what God tells us to do when we become aware of such things. We are to direct our hate toward Satan, not the person who caved in to Satan's suggestion to do evil. We are to pray for the people who sinned in whatever evil it is they consented to.

Judges have an important job to do to protect the public against evildoers through restitution (if it is reasonably possible) or through imprisonment so they can't be a threat against the public. But vengeance is up to God, not us.

The Charles Ng case offers a good example of why moral people need to remember who the judge is. Ng was wanted in the United States for a series of brutal rapes and murders but was caught shoplifting in Calgary, Alberta. Because he could be executed for what he had done, the Canadian government was involved in a long legal battle over his extradition.

Using money from taxpayers to protect a known criminal is enough to cause bitter anger and resentment against the government. People directed their anger and resentment toward Ng and toward the government, just as Satan would want. However, God said let the evil, wicked, and filth continue on in their evil, wicked, and filthy ways (Revelation 22:11). God said this because all any of them are doing is arranging their own demise for judgment day.

Let it go; let God deal with whatever evil is at work. Focus only on being loving and pray for strength to be lovingly kind and compassionate toward all others to the best of your ability because any wrong anyone else has done is being dealt with by our Father in heaven. Judgment will come in due time.

Charles Ng's childhood was terrible. Who knows what he would have been like otherwise? Did the

efforts made on his behalf by the Canadian government affect his outlook on life? We don't know but
our heavenly Father, Jehovah God Almighty, knows
because He ponders everyone's heart. So do not turn
on the news to find out whom to be mad at and feel
hateful toward because if you do, all you are really
doing is supporting Satan's cause and stressing yourself out.

Back in the late 1970s, I was listening to the
news about Mohammad Reza Pahlavi, shah of Iran,
which routinely depicted him as a bloodthirsty tyrant,
a ruthless money-hungry tormenter of his own people. But in 2015, while revising this book, I decided to
investigate, and what I learned about him surprised
me.

When he became the Shah of Iran, his kingdom
(formerly known as Persia) was floundering. Bandits
dominated the land, literacy was at 1 percent, and
women, under archaic Islamic dictates, had no rights.
As the country's king, he took Iran out of the dark
ages to become the world's second largest producer
of oil. He modernized the roads, built schools colleges and universities at his own expense. He granted
women equal rights, not to accommodate feminism
but to end archaic brutalization. He was pro-Western
and anti-communist. He was a highly respected ally of

the United States and Britain. He encouraged independent cultivation—citizens owning their own farms. He constructed dams to irrigate Iran's arid land, and he donated 500,000 acres of crown land to 2,500 farmers to farm as they pleased (private enterprise). The result of his blessing on his people resulted in Iran becoming 90 percent self-sufficient in food production.

The national currency was stable for fifteen years, inspiring French economist Andre Piettre to call Iran a country of "growth without inflation." There is a lot more I could say about the good I learned from the history on what the shah of Iran was doing and planning for his country. But getting back to the bottom line, does his track record fit the stories depicted of him in the last couple of years of his rulership of Iran?

Ways and actions speak louder than words, so I question what was going on to get rid of him. Corrupt people are continually manipulating to get wealth. He was against communism. He abolished Islamic brutality of women. So he definitely had enemies determined to crush him.

Who then supported Ayatollah Khomeini, enabling him to overthrow the last shah of Iran? And what has become of that country since?

My mother often said, "Every man believes he is right in his own eye." Therefore, I decided I needed to look into the biography of Ayatollah Khomeini to come to an understanding of his reasoning.

As a young man, Khomeini had a relentless desire to educate himself in Islamic law. Sharia is believed by Muslims to represent divine law as revealed in the Quran and the Sunnah (the teaching and practices of the Islamic prophet Muhammad). In his study of politics and religion, he determined that politically derived laws were bad for people; and when you see our Western culture's relaxed laws on abortion, prostitution, bribery through lobbying, etc., it is easy to see how he could conclude that the best thing for mankind would be a law from a higher power than man. He thought the best antidote to Western immorality was Sharia law. However, it does not make sense to me that Khomeini was against allowing the masses access to the same education he had sought for himself. After about 10 years of his rule, about 70 percent of the educated people of Iran had left the country.

With the return to Sharia law, everything changed. Men were in violation of the law if they wore shorts in that hot climate, and women had to cover their hair. Men and women were not allowed to swim or sunbathe together. Western movies and alcoholic drinks were banned. The economy floundered under his oppression, and the country went backwards.

And Khomeini implemented a mass hunt to find and execute anyone suspected of being opposed to his dictatorship.

The God of Christianity is all about loving everyone and *praying* for those who have allowed the little voice of evil to dominate their thoughts. Killing people for not agreeing with what you believe is lording yourself over others, the antithesis of what God wanted us to do.

As Ayatollah Khomeini's health declined, before he died, he rescinded some of the strict laws he had imposed on the people. Perhaps he had started to realize he had erred in his ways. I don't know. However, there is one thing I do know for sure, and that is that every male and female was knit together in a mother's womb by our loving Creator, God Almighty. Therefore, every female is a daughter of God's, and as such, they are to be equally respected. This means equal rights to dignity, education, and choice. Therefore, the Sharia laws on gender do not reflect the merciful and loving Creator so clearly described in the Holy Bible.

The Holy Bible teaches us to tell others about the love of God Almighty and His Son, Jesus Christ, and it says if they choose not to believe, *leave them be.* The living God Almighty of the Holy Bible says He, and He alone, will ponder the righteousness of every individual man and woman's heart. How can the flawed rightfully judge others? Only God can be the judge because only He can truly ponder anyone's heart.

In the end, Satan will always fail because insanity cannot triumph over sanity. Therefore, don't let Satan's insanity rule you, my friend.

To Be Ladies and Gentlemen

The Holy Bible tells us that men are the stronger sex. However, it also instructs us about what this means. It does *not* mean men are to domineer over women. It *does* mean he must accept the larger part of some responsibilities. A very important part of his responsibility is to provide a good example by being a decent, honest, and caring citizen. A gentleman is a righteous man, considerate toward all others, and a hardworking guardian who serves those under his care.

In most family situations, meeting these responsibilities will require a tremendous amount of endurance and the ability to remain calm and thoughtful. To do this job well means a man must put the concerns, needs, and safety of others ahead of his own. Although this role is taxing, it is always regarded as a privilege by men who love being sincere gentlemen to the best of their ability. It does not take a macho man of muscles to be a gentleman. However, it does take a man with a clean thinking mind and a caring heart to be a strong gentleman worthy of respect.

Women have been in a fight against men for equal rights for over a century. One reason is that they have recognized how men's hearts have cooled off; they were not treating women with the respect they deserved.

For too long, far too many men have used false politeness as a lure, and too many men have exploited and abused those they should care about. Women have revolted against chauvinism, against being over-run by men who have preyed on them. The revolt has had its own cooling effect, making it more difficult for people to trust one another to do the right thing and to be confident about doing the right thing. Men who do deserve the title gentlemen have become a fading breed. Instead of men having respect for others, who would in turn honor them back with respect, we have a world polluted with spiteful deceivers as Satan's time to control this earth is coming to an end.

The power-hungry and self-gratifying attitude modeled by our leaders has affected all of society. The Old Testament describes this; both 1 Kings and 2 Kings are about the natures of good and evil kings and show how the nation changed to follow their leader. It is a consistent pattern that played out over thousands of years with the kings of Israel, a pattern that is consistent today in all nations. If a leader sets a good example by the way he acts, then his followers will also set a good example to those under them. And if a leader sets a bad example by the way he acts, then his followers will too.

Men started treating women with less and less respect, so women started treating men the same. Now children are following their example by treating neither of their parents with respect. This "no respect" pattern is exactly what Satan wants. *A good salesman is someone who can tell you to go to hell in such a way that you will be looking forward to the trip.*

How blind are we when allowing ourselves to be taken in this way? Why are we allowing Satan to use us to destroy our governments, our neighborhoods, and even our own families with his constant little bad voice suggestions in our heads? We must wake up and realize who our enemy is. It is not our fellow man; it is Satan using his influence to blind us and our fellow man.

Satan has always done everything he can to blind us. He wants to convince us that God Almighty is stopping us from the ultimate enjoyment of all that we deserve and professes that he, with his demon advocates, are our friends, just like he did in the garden of Eden.

Satan's manipulations have caused the true spirit of being ladies and gentlemen to almost become extinct. A lot of children, and many adults, no longer know what it means to act like ladies and gentlemen. Study the Holy Scriptures yourself and, with others to fortify your mind to become a pillar of strength for righteousness sake. Do not let Satan control your attitude to destroy your good spirit of righteous morality and enjoyment of your sexuality as a gentleman or a lady.

Going it Alone

Loneliness is a sad situation that tens of millions of men and women today live with because of Satan's effect on their lives, crippling their hope for a truly fulfilling heterosexual relationship. This situation can be changed for anyone anywhere who will change their ways that are keeping them condemned to this type of insecure and lonely lifestyle. There are two ways to do anything. One is to choose the path set out by our heavenly Father—the loving way that always comes with his blessings. Any other way can fail at any time. If you sincerely want your love relationship (or any other situation in your life) to improve, then do it by God's method.

I spent many years looking for someone to be my companion in marriage. I dreamt up and tried many different strategies to find the right woman and suffered a lot of disappointment. Then one day when I was twenty-six, I felt like giving up completely. For the first time, I prayed about it. "Lord God, please let it be that I will never become involved with another person unless they are the right person for me to share the rest of my life with." I had cast my concern on God to deal with, and I did not try to pursue it any more.

About seven months after praying that prayer and starting to trust in Almighty God rather than myself, some peculiar circumstances happened, bringing me into contact with the young lady who became my wife. Today, some forty years later, I can only say that God must have arranged everything to answer our prayers.

Many times, my mother came up against what looked like insurmountable problems. She would pray to God to help her and then go back to work at whatever she was doing in faith and prayer. Often, unusual events would start taking place, leading up to a surprising resolution to the problem. Numerous times as a child, I listened to my mother recounting our family history, ending her reminiscences with, "When you have done all that you can do, then God will do the rest."

These are faith-filled words we can depend on regarding anything from protection and health to finance and love. Just state with conviction from God's living promises in the Holy Bible what you want and have patience and faith that it will come to pass.

The Spirit is still in us, to some degree, to practice being ladies and gentlemen, sympathetic and compassionate for each other and others. It's the little spirit voice of goodness that grows if we listen to it or if we ignore it, dwindles until we can't hear it anymore. However, because of the overwhelming evil that surrounds us, many men, women, and children find themselves still falling victim to the bad little voice of Satan's chants against their own better judgment with statements like:

- I quit.
- I'm out of here.
- I wish you would listen to me.
- You blame me all the time.
- You tick me off.
- So what, it's not my problem.

It's always I, I, I, and me, me, me. Selfish statements are not in the will of God's love for us. Marriage is not all smooth sailing. There will be disagreements, but if you will apply God's kind of love, you will come to agreements that will strengthen your love toward your spouse and everyone else, whether we know them or not. Avoid using Satan's chants, which can only promote destructive evil.

We all need to get to know about our Creator, Jehovah God Almighty personally as our loving Father in heaven. This is required to feel confident within ourselves and that God sincerely loves us.

When any one of us evaluates what we want in a relationship, we will all have to admit that it is the same. We all must admit that our most treasured desire is to be with a person of the opposite sex who we would know, without question, sincerely honors, respects, and loves us, and who will keep themselves attractive and sacred for us to the best of their ability for the rest of their life.

However, there is only one way for anyone to have hope of this desire coming true for them. That is, that they must practice being that same way themselves first, and always. Therefore, give Jesus Christ's message to love your neighbor as you love yourself, serious concern in your heart. Guard against sliding into the immoral degenerate ways that evil spirits continually try to influence society toward. Become conscientious of every aspect of society as it is explained in this book. And start practicing the good advice it offers you to become a decent lady or gentle-men forevermore. This is a prime concern if you want to get the most happiness you can out of your life and your resurrected life to come. Caring for yourself both hygienically and morally as a decent lady or gentle-men is the only way you can profit from an incredible love experience in your marriage.

Your honorary worth as a lady or a gentleman all depends on the state you make up your mind to live by. So why not take time out in a quiet place, with-out any distractions and interference from electronic entertainment, to stop and think about how you need to change.

Heterosexual Partnership's Power

Proverbs 8 is about my friend Wisdom. She is God's friend too, and she should be everyone's best friend. The Book of Proverbs is filled with valuable information to help everyone become ladies and gentlemen. Therefore, the following is important to consider:

The Holy Bible refers to God as masculine and Wisdom as feminine. In the book of Proverbs, it emphasizes several times that wisdom is a she. That tells me it's an important fact to note because of how many times it is restated, and the other fact stressed is that God created everything, He created with Wisdom at His side.

Brain wave testing has shown that men and women's brains function differently. Men focus on one part of the brain for a logical truth to answer each question. Women being asked the same questions scan their whole brain to reason their answers to the questions. Therefore, wisdom gives more to consider to get the best results.

The Bible states in Proverbs 3:17, "All Wisdoms' ways are pleasantness and peace." That's a truly feminine touch of a good lady. All God's ways are logical truth. That is a truly masculine touch of a good gentleman. Therefore, noble ladies and gentlemen in heterosexual harmony is awesome. No wonder Satan strives to brainwash people to prevent and destroy heterosexual marriages.

Start Walking Tall for What Is Right

Your decision to walk tall for what is righteous, for what is good, for what is morally decent will garner respect of others regardless of their own behavior. We see this when only one person in a group refuses to join in foul-mouthed, vulgar, and malicious discussions and instead continues to speak respectfully.

Our society has embraced entertainment from cartoons to music to movies that make violence seem amusing or admirable. People immerse themselves in realistic and violent video games. Hour after hour, day after day, they desensitize themselves to killing hundreds or even thousands of people. These war games are teaching children to kill spontaneously without ever considering the consequences of what they are doing. And we need to jolt ourselves into awareness of what we have allowed ourselves to become immersed in. How can this desensitizing influence mentor anything good in anyone?

Everyone needs to know the good news about our Creator and His happiness for all mankind that is soon to come. That is why I wrote this book, to hopefully help children and everyone else to know there is a good potential purpose in everyone's future. All you have to do is start living the way our Creator has shown us. His operating manual clearly explains how men and women become polished ladies and gentlemen. It is never too late to be a good role model for your children, no matter what age they are, or for the other people in your life.

The best example I can think of for this is the Apostle Paul. Before he became an apostle, he was in the business of killing Christians because of the way he was raised. Then when he learned he was wrong, he changed to being the most outspoken Christian of all the apostles. Many knew what he was before, but after they heard what he had to say later, they changed to become Christians also.

Any one of us can lead the way if we judge our motives and correct our attitudes to the righteous ways of honorable ladies and gentlemen.

Really Making Love

To really be making love means to fulfill all aspects that make up the spirit of being a loving person. Although many people think of making love as sharing pleasure in foreplay and sexual intercourse, these activities only contribute to making intimate love complete. The state of our attitude toward everything else in our life will determine whether or not we are really making love. We must do everything we possibly can to minimize stress and promote happiness in the lives of everyone we affect.

First, we need to examine how fair we try to be in our dealings with people. Are you always trying to get the most for the least? This type of an approach to life generates anxiety on everyone you have any transaction with. For example, let's say your vehicle is failing. Knowing it is about to start costing you a lot of money for repairs, you still want to get as much as you can by selling it without honestly disclosing the problems. With this type of attitude, are you showing any kind of compassion for your neighbors of this world? The car has been of good service to you, so be honest about the car; sell it at a price that gives the buyer some leeway for potential expenses that are likely to come up and pray that it will be a blessing to them.

The statement "it is better to give than receive" holds true in everything you do in life.

Are you a businessperson who tries to underbid your competition? You know it would be fair and sensible to charge more, but you're more interested in getting all the business for yourself. If you do this, aren't you stealing customers from others who are trying to charge a reasonable and fair business price for the jobs? What true advantage is there in underbidding your competitors when making it difficult for them to compete also means taking the risk of ruining your own business too?

In 1975, when I was working as a landscape contractor in Prince George, British Columbia, I was charging 25 percent more than the other contractors for putting in sod lawns. They were charging 15 cents per square foot while I was charging 20 cents per square foot, and still I had been struggling for four years to make ends meet, in part, because I also paid my employees more to the best of my ability. A starving wage does not promote happiness.

One of the other contractors called me, wanting all of us to come to a meeting. I thought yes, it is high time we did. At the meeting, I was shocked to learn that in Vancouver, landscapers were charging far more than I was at 44 cents per square foot for sod lawns. No wonder we were struggling. The decision at the end of the meeting was that they were all going to charge $0.20 per square foot. Knowing this was still too low, I set my new price at 26 cents per square foot.

All of us relied on one sod farmer who promised he would deliver sod to us at $0.50 per yard (5.5 cents per square foot). After everyone had bid on the jobs for that summer, the sod farmer said he changed his mind. The price would be $0.75 per yard (8.3 cents per square foot) delivered and $0.50 per yard in the field. That meant we would have to find our own transportation or pay 50 percent more. So it was another year of struggling to make ends meet.

About halfway through July, one of the landscapers saw me on a jobsite and came over to talk to me. We talked about how difficult the ambush price raise had made things, and he asked me how much I was charging. When I told him, his face fell. He told me that everyone figured with everyone else charging 20 cents per square foot if they kept their price at 15 cents they would end up with all the business.

Of course, he didn't; people were willing to pay the more sensible rate. I managed to survive another year. Others went bankrupt, trying to steal business away from those trying to charge a fair and reasonable rate and pay employees a decent wage.

Years later, long after I'd given up landscaping to work as a power engineer, I needed someone to take on a project in my own yard. I went to the park where young people hung out and asked some of them if they were interested in replacing a weed patch with a seeded lawn. I hired a crew of four and was telling my neighbors what good workers they were. They asked me how much I was paying them. I said $18 an hour. My neighbors couldn't understand why I was paying unskilled labor more than the minimum wage, which was about $9 or $10 per hour. I just smiled and said, "They're happy and so am I with what they are doing." *Really making love produces contentment both ways.*

When the job was finished, I asked them for their time sheet. I looked at it and said, "You came here at 8:00 each day and left at 5:00, right? That's not 7.5 hours per day."

They said the rest of the time was their coffee breaks and lunch hour, when we treated them to barbeque lunches. So I asked them, "When you were having your lunch, weren't you refueling to continue working for me?"

They looked puzzled and said, "Ya, I guess so."

I said, "Well then, you were working for me, right?" They agreed and I paid them for nine hours per day.

Were they happy? You know they were. Was I happy? Well, that job was done years ago, and my family and friends have enjoyed a lush green lawn since then, so you know, I am exceptionally happy.

I got my example of how to be as an employer from a parable shared by Jesus in Matthew 20:1–16 on generosity, and I encourage you to take a moment with the Holy Bible to read these verses.

Promote happiness and you will receive the same. Promote happiness by cheerfully being generous when you can to the poor. Having this type of an attitude generates a joy in you, the perpetual bliss that is enjoyed by benevolent people. Really making love is all about doing what you can to be good to your spouse, children, and your neighbors of this world.

This is also the way a relationship should work between a mature and loving couple. They should be loyally committed with a sincere desire to live their lives for each other in marriage. Only then can sexual intercourse between them make the love between them complete. It is their loving gift that they sacredly share with each other.

God's kind of love is doing something for the good of others. We must understand the fundamentals required to have fulfilled the act of really making love.

Some of the traits that must become part of your personal nature in order to be a great lover are charity, compassion, patience, and forgiveness toward everyone. These essential characteristics are all easy to understand. No degree in philosophy is required to become skilled in them. All that is required of you is to respect and follow the advice of your Father in heaven, Jehovah God Almighty. If you place your confidence in the nature of true love, you will be filled with good common sense throughout your lifetime. What you gain is far beyond what a degree in philosophical theories could ever provide. The simplicity of true love means becoming a great love maker, and it is accessible to anyone. The Holy Bible clearly shows it is within the grasp of anyone who wants it.

You need to first develop a love for truthfulness, cleanliness, and good moral principles. You either choose righteous ways that nourish life, or you choose unrighteous ways that lead to death. Your chosen attitude determines whether you are a great lover, like God, or not, as described in Romans 8:12–16. There it says,

> Therefore, brothers we have an obligation—but it is not to the sinful nature, to live according to it.
> For if you live according to the sinful nature, you will die; but if by the Spirit you put to death the misdeeds of the body, you will live, because those who are led by the Spirit of God, are sons of God.
> For you did not receive a spirit that makes you a slave again to fear, but you receive the Spirit of sonship. And, by him we cry "Abba, Father."
> The Spirit himself testifies with our spirit, that we are God's children.

Do not misunderstand God's declared promise here regarding those who live by God's spirit of love in them. Those who do are God's children. If you are wondering what exactly that means, the answer is in the next verse:

> Now if we are children, then we
> are heirs—heirs of God and co-heirs
> with Christ, if indeed we share with
> his suffering in order that we may
> also share in his glory.

Are there any limits to God's wealth? No, not at all. So why would you ever want to reject God's offer to adopt you as His child to share in His wealth?

Therefore, be on guard to prevent that little voice of evil spirits from enticing you to surrender back to their wicked ways. Once you have made it your business to be a merciful, kind, and loving person toward all others, remain steadfast to your commitment no matter what little thing evil tries to do to recruit you back to its old way. This is vitally important because of what it states at James 2:10,

> For whoever shall keep the
> whole law, and yet offend in one
> point, he is guilty of all.

Some, considering the way they have lived life so far, feel condemned to hell regardless of what they do in the future. However, this is not necessarily true. Some people have lived selfishly until they were in their mid-twenties, then have gone through a dramatic experience that caused them to realize how wrong they have been, just as the Apostle Paul did. He described himself as being the chief of sinners who turned away from his past life and never looked back.

The way you have lived your life so far is not necessarily a waste, *unless you choose for it to have been so.* If you develop a strong hatred for the bad way you have been in the past, you will be able to make a dramatic change for the better. Sometimes the impact of this reality makes such a dramatic change in people's reasoning that they suddenly absolutely devote themselves to totally change from the irrational way they have been living in the past.

I know many people who are now Christians who were heavily involved with crime, prostitution, and many other unloving ways before they came to know Jesus Christ as their Lord and Savior. They have managed to abandon their past life completely and committed to living righteously. And I believe anyone who sincerely wants to change for the better can, and that God will love you for making this change; the Apostle Paul is not the only example in the Holy Bible.

To make loving your lifetime way, you must live by the righteous laws as written in the Holy Bible. These laws were put there not to enslave us or deprive us of any worthwhile joy but to protect us and enrich every aspect of our lives. It's the rewarding power of living a truly benevolent life with respect for all.

Throughout history, and especially today, people who mean others no harm have been put down for trying to live as an example of the righteous good moral ways of wisdom from the Holy Bible. They are laughed at, tormented, and ridiculed by heathens who know God but defy His existence and worth. Do not let them bring you down, for they know you are right when you live by righteousness. They hate you for trying to be good, as they know they should be. For they know you are a precious jewel of the Almighty Creator of the universe when you show mercy, kindness, understanding, and forgiveness toward others. They know you are a great lover who is really making love.

If you want to count yourself dead to sin as you devote yourself to living a benevolent life under Jesus Christ's grace, His grace pardons us of our present sinful nature as we struggle to avoid rebecoming servants to sin. To learn the full depth of what Jesus's gift of grace means to you, read the Book of Romans in the New Testament and study it with others who know about Jesus Christ's gracious gift of eternal life. The eternal life inheritance of making love will ever increase and never end as we complete this life and go on to our resurrected life promised by God Almighty. It has been proven that our Creator is in the resurrection business, as is shown by the evidence discussed in the second chapter of this book. So choose this day whom you will serve. Sin or righteousness? There is no third option. The battle against being taken by Satan is well worth fighting because righteousness is an ever-increasing envelopment of wealth that will never end.

If you are ready to take the first step to change your life to a righteous one, then pray this sinner's prayer:

Lord God Almighty, I acknowledge that I have sinned against you. I am sorry for my sins. From this moment on, I want to turn from my sins to live for and serve you, Jesus Christ of Nazareth, as my Lord and Savior. Amen.

If you were sincere about this, welcome to Jesus's family.

I pray, Jehovah God, our heavenly Father who art in heaven, thank you for your many gracious mercies. Thank you for the glory of all your marvelous creations of nature which you have freely given to us to enjoy and to learn from. Please, let it be that this book about your creation and love for us will not cause any man to stumble and fall but rather will be a blessing to all who read it and to all with whom they share it. I ask these things with loving hope in your only begotten Son, Jesus Christ of Nazareth, who is our Lord and Savior. Amen.

If this book has made sense to you and you would like to help someone change their ways for the better, send them a copy of this book. Bless others as I have hopefully blessed you with my book. It should be in everybody's library to refer to. We all know people who need help with circumstances like divorce depression, addictions, and abuses of every nature. Some of us know people in cults and gangs and incarcerated people that I also wrote this book for to hopefully help them see the light of what is right.

Take care and God bless.

Website: gshasa.org or gshasa.ca

Email: contact@gshasa.ca

Good Sexual Hygiene and Spiritual Attitude is easy to understand and a fast-track motivator on good human ethics.

Notes

Notes

Notes

Notes

About the Author

Anthony A. Morris (a.k.a. Tony) and his wife have been married for forty-two years and have three children, two adults and a twelve-year-old. He has worn many different hats in his life. Upon finishing school, he became a landscape contractor for the next five years and took up power steam engineering the first winter after graduation, which later became his main career for life. He also worked as a volunteer firefighter, ambulance attendant, school bus driver, and he and his wife became active foster parents off and on shortly after they were married. All this came with many new experiences to base life's values on.

When he was in junior high, they said nobody had written a book to teach sex education; therefore, he started writing a script for this when their older children started becoming teens. The more he worked on it, the more he realized how much more was needed to properly address that subject. Thus, he wrote this book on ethical values that wasn't finished until thirty-five years later after retiring.

CPSIA information can be obtained
at www.ICGtesting.com
Printed in the USA
BVHW070304031222
653283BV00001B/4